THE
UNSEEN
SEEN

DON LITTON

authorHOUSE®

AuthorHouse™
1663 Liberty Drive
Bloomington, IN 47403
www.authorhouse.com
Phone: 1 (800) 839-8640

Published by AuthorHouse 08/06/2019

ISBN: 978-1-7283-2225-4 (sc)
ISBN: 978-1-7283-2224-7 (e)

Print information available on the last page.

Any people depicted in stock imagery provided by Getty Images are models,
and such images are being used for illustrative purposes only.
Certain stock imagery © Getty Images.

This book is printed on acid-free paper.

Unless otherwise indicated, all scripture quotations are from The Holy Bible, English
Standard Version® (ESV®). Copyright ©2001 by Crossway Bibles, a division
of Good News Publishers. Used by permission. All rights reserved.

Scripture quotations marked KJV are from the Holy Bible, King James Version
(Authorized Version). First published in 1611. Quoted from the KJV Classic
Reference Bible, Copyright © 1983 by The Zondervan Corporation.

Scripture quotations marked NASB are taken from the New American Standard Bible®, Copyright © 1960,
1962, 1963, 1968, 1971, 1972, 1973, 1975, 1977, 1995 by The Lockman Foundation. Used by permission.

The Holy Bible, New English Bible, (NEB), Oxford University Press, 1970.

Scripture quotations marked NIV are taken from the Holy Bible, New International
Version®. NIV®. Copyright © 1973, 1978, 1984 by International Bible Society.
Used by permission of Zondervan. All rights reserved. [Biblica]

Scripture quotations marked NLT are taken from the Holy Bible, New Living
Translation, copyright © 1996, 2004, 2007. Used by permission of Tyndale House
Publishers, Inc. Carol Stream, Illinois 60188. All rights reserved. Website

Scripture quotations marked RSV are taken from the Revised Standard Version of
the Bible, copyright © 1946, 1952, 1971 by the Division of Christian Education of the
National Council of the Churches of Christ in the USA. Used by permission.

The Holy Bible, The New Testament in Modern English, (Philips), 1958.

CONTENTS

ACKNOWLEDGMENT

Writing a book was harder than I thought and more rewarding than I could have ever imagined. No one in life does anything worthwhile alone. So, in my case I have several special people to acknowledge. My wife, Janice, has kept me comforted and has for years put up with my crazy schedule, mainly my daytime and nighttime hours being in reverse order. Her love for Christ and me has allowed me great freedom to execute my calling. The members of Friendship Baptist Church in Fishville, La "endured my preaching and teaching" for 13 yrs, until January of 2018. They were a captive audience for my stories and not so humorous jokes; they would even groan when I began to tell them.

I would not have made it this far in my book had not my sister, Rita Litton Ellis, spent countless hours reading, correcting, and revising sentences and paragraphs of my manuscript. More importantly, I thank God for the journey, age 73, and to have KNOWN HIM for 58 years. Being a reborn Christian, the Lord has guided me with HIS eye and it has been an insane walk with HIM. Only a foolish man would say I know a lot about God because in my case the more I have learned about HIM, the less I realized I know.

INTRODUCTION

The church has been lulled to sleep and in many cases, is oblivious to the battle raging against its very existence. But we must awaken and return to the core identity of the church as stated by Jesus:

Mark 11:17 - "And he taught, saying unto them, Is it not written, My house shall be called of all nations the house of prayer? but ye have made it a den of thieves" **(KJV)**.

It is time to put on the whole armor of God and embrace the mantle of intercession to stand in the gap for the souls of our nation.

There is an unseen battle raging against Christians. We cannot see it with our natural eyes, yet at times we can feel its effect. The enemy is walking around as a roaring lion seeking to destroy us. He wants to kill your dreams and destroy your destiny. We must learn to be armed, ready and engaged in the battle for our marriages, our children and our country as well as the nations of the earth. It is time to put on our spiritual armor and take a stand against the enemy. God has promised that no weapon formed against us shall prosper (Charisma, 2018):

Isaiah 54:17 - "No weapon that is formed against thee shall prosper; and every tongue that shall rise against thee in judgment thou shalt condemn. This is the heritage of the servants of the LORD, and their righteousness is of me, saith the LORD" **(KJV)**.

Paul admonishes us to put on the whole armor of God in order to withstand the evil forces of hell:

Ephesians 6:11 - "Put on the whole armour of God, that ye may be able to stand against the wiles of the devil" (**KJV**).

Many would argue that since Jesus died on the cross, everything is already finished and the devil is defeated. Although the devil has ultimately been defeated, he still seeks to kill, steal and destroy. God has given us the responsibility to enforce the finished work of the cross. Just because we are saved does not mean we are immune to the attacks of the enemy. We must be infused with the strength of the Lord to overcome the assault of the enemy. We have priority access to the power of the Father to reverse every wicked plan, plot, and scheme against our lives. Do not fight in your own strength:

II Corinthians 10:4 - "The weapons of our warfare are not carnal, but mighty through God to the pulling down of strongholds" (**KJV**).

The Bible speaks about the reality of a conflict, we face as believers, and we popularly call that conflict "spiritual warfare." The apostle Paul explained that our perception of the unseen world is presently somewhat obscured:

I Corinthians 13:12 - "For now we see only a reflection as in a mirror; then we shall see face to face. Now I know in part; then I shall know fully, even as I am fully known" (**NIV**).

God wants us to believe in things unseen purely by faith, because of what He says about them in His Word. If we could see all that is around us in the spirit world, it would be too easy to believe. There is only one God Almighty, one Creator of all things, but there are countless millions of lesser spiritual beings whom He has created, who operate within the bounds God has established for them. May God open our eyes to the things of the Spirit.

CHAPTER 1

UNSEEN SEEN

(The Spirit World)

A dog whistle works by playing a single note that is audible to dogs but not to humans. Humans can hear sounds between 64 and 23,000 Hz, while dogs can hear sounds between 67 and 45,000 Hz. Cats can hear an even broader range of sounds, between 45 and 64,000 Hz. The larger numbers represent higher pitched sounds, and the lower numbers correspond to lower sounds. Different species of animals hear different ranges of sound. If a sound occurs at a higher pitch than the animal is capable of hearing, the animal cannot hear it with their ears.

There is an unseen world all around us. We can only detect the existence of certain things in the universe when they affect something around it. We cannot see the wind, but we can watch as tree boughs bend, and leaves flutter to the ground. We cannot see gravity, but we can discern that there is a force pulling dropped objects toward the earth.

The Bible tells us that a spiritual world does exist, and we may sometimes encounter realities from that realm, both good and bad:

Hebrews 13:2 - "Do not neglect to show hospitality to strangers, for thereby some have entertained angels unawares" (**RSV**).

Ephesians 6:12 - "For we are not contending against flesh and blood, but against the principalities, against the powers, against the world rulers of this present darkness, against the spiritual hosts of wickedness in the heavenly places" (**RSV**).

Because of this, we are encouraged to be watchful, prayerful, and prepared. Just as God rules the world we see, He also rules the unseen world.

What is the "UNSEEN" world? The Bible teaches that an unseen world of spirits surrounds us. It is both real and powerful. The magic of Pharaoh's servants was genuine, but the power God gave Moses was greater (**Exodus 7 to Exodus 8**). While various people, some with and some without God's consent, may actively engage this invisible world, no one's authority can compare to that of Jesus:

Matthew 8:14-17 - "When Jesus came into Peter's home, He saw his mother-in-law lying sick in bed with a fever. He touched her hand, and the fever left her; and she got up and waited on Him. When evening came, they brought to Him many who were demon-possessed; and He cast out the spirits with a word, and healed all who were ill. *This was* to fulfill what was spoken through Isaiah the prophet: "He Himself took our infirmities and carried away our diseases" (**NASB**).

Jesus gave similar power to His twelve apostles:

Matthew 10:1 - "Jesus summoned His twelve disciples and gave them authority over unclean spirits, to cast them out, and to heal every kind of disease and every kind of sickness" (**NASB**).

Acts 3:3-8 - "When he saw Peter and John about to go into the temple, he began asking to receive alms. But Peter, along with John, fixed his gaze on him and said, "Look at us!" And he began to give them his attention, expecting to receive something from them. But Peter said, "I do not possess silver and gold, but what I do have I give to you: In the name of Jesus Christ the Nazarene, walk!" And seizing him by the right hand, he raised him up; and immediately his feet and his ankles were strengthened. With a leap he stood upright and began to walk; and he entered the temple with them, walking and leaping and praising God" (**RSV**).

Acts 6:8 - "And Stephen, full of grace and power, was performing great wonders and signs among the people" (**RSV**).

Acts 8:12-13 - "But when they believed Philip preaching the good news about the kingdom of God and the name of Jesus Christ, they were being baptized, men and women alike. Even Simon himself believed; and after being baptized, he continued on with Philip, and as he observed signs and great miracles taking place, he was constantly amazed" (**NASB**).

Acts 19:11-12 - "God was performing extraordinary miracles by the hands of Paul, so that handkerchiefs or aprons were even carried from his body to the sick, and the diseases left them and the evil spirits went out" (**NASB**).

More damaging than physical ills are the false teachings promoted by demons through people:

I Timothy 4:1 - "But the Spirit explicitly says that in later times some will fall away from the faith, paying attention to deceitful spirits and doctrines of demons" (**NASB**).

While there are bad spirits, there are also good spirits known as angels. They sometimes assist and even visit God's people:

Hebrews 1:13-14 - "But to which of the angels has He ever said, 'SIT AT MY RIGHT HAND, UNTIL I MAKE YOUR ENEMIES A FOOTSTOOL FOR YOUR FEET'? Are they not all ministering spirits, sent out to render service for the sake of those who will inherit salvation?" (**NASB**).

The Bible teaches the existence of an immaterial, spiritual reality, unseen by human eyes. The physical reality is evident for all to see, although some doubt the existence of a material universe, too! The Bible says that the spiritual realm consists of both good, God and the holy angels, and evil, the devil and his demons. Demons are fallen angels who rebelled against God and were thrown out of heaven (Kruse, 1999):

Ezekiel 28:11-17 - "You were the seal of perfection, full of wisdom and perfect in beauty. You were in Eden, the garden of God; every precious stone adorned you: carnelian, chrysolite and emerald, topaz, onyx and jasper, lapis lazuli, turquoise and beryl. Your settings and mountings were made of gold; on the day you were created they were prepared. You were anointed as a guardian cherub, for so ordained you. You were on the holy mount of God; you walked among the fiery stones. You were blameless in your ways from the day you were created till wickedness was found in you. Through your widespread trade you were filled with violence, and you sinned. So I drove you in disgrace from the mount of God, and I expelled you, guardian cherub, from among the fiery stones. Your heart became proud on account of your beauty, and you corrupted your wisdom because of your splendor. So I threw you to the earth; I made a spectacle of you before kings" (**NIV**).

Isaiah 14:12-15 - "How you have fallen from heaven, morning star, son of the dawn! You have been cast down to the earth, you who once laid low the nations! You said in your heart, "I will ascend to the heavens; I will raise my throne above the stars of God; I will sit enthroned on the mount of assembly, on the utmost heights of Mount Zap hon. I will ascend above the tops of the clouds; I will make myself like the Most High." But you are brought down to the realm of the dead, to the depths of the pit. How you have fallen from heaven, morning star, son of the dawn! You have been cast down to the earth, you who once laid low the nations! You said in your heart, "I will ascend to the heavens; I will raise my throne above the stars of God; I will sit enthroned on the mount of assembly, on the utmost heights of Mount Zaphon. I will ascend above the tops of the clouds; I will make myself like the Most High." But you are brought down to the realm of the dead, to the depths of the pit" (**NIV**).

Revelation 12:7-9 - "Then war broke out in heaven. Michael and his angels fought against the dragon, and the dragon and his angels fought back. But he was not strong enough, and they lost their place in heaven. The great dragon was hurled down—that ancient serpent called the devil, or Satan, who leads the whole world astray. He was hurled to the earth, and his angels with him" (**NIV**).

The Bible also teaches that humans were created by God in His image, which means we have a spiritual component.

Genesis 1:27 - "So God created mankind in his own image, in the image of God he created them; male and female he created them" (**NIV**).

We are more than physical entities; we possess a soul/spirit destined for eternity. Even though the spiritual realm is invisible to the physical eye, we are connected to it, and what goes on in the spiritual realm directly affects our physical world. The best testimonial evidence for a spiritual realm is the Bible itself. Historians, both Christian and non-Christian, agree that the historical authenticity of the Bible is strong. Jesus claimed to be God's, Son, the One who came down from heaven. He made this fact quite clear (Got Questions, 2013).

John 8:23 - "But he continued, 'You are from below; I am from above. You are of this world; I am not of this world'" (**NIV**).

The Bible recounts numerous encounters that people had with the spiritual realm. Jesus cast demons out of people regularly, healed the sick by speaking to them, miraculously fed thousands of people, and spoke with people who should be dead: Moses and Elijah.

Matthew 17:1-3 - "After six days Jesus took with him Peter, James and John the brother of James, and led them up a high mountain by themselves. There he was transfigured before them. His face shone like the sun, and his clothes became as white as the light. Just then there appeared before them Moses and Elijah, talking with Jesus" (**NIV**).

The Unseen World Carries More Truth and Reality Than the Physical World.

There is an unseen world. The Bible is very clear that this physical world we live in isn't the end all of God's creation. There is a spiritual realm that we can't see with our physical eyes.

Colossians 1:15-16 - "Who is the image of the invisible God, the firstborn of every creature: For by him were all things created, that are in heaven, and that are in earth, visible and invisible, whether they be thrones, or dominions, or principalities, or powers: all things were created by him, and for him" **(KJV)**.

This passage of scripture tells us that Jesus is the visible image of an invisible God and that I Him, God created all things in the "heavenly realms and on earth." We discover also in this passage that there are "thrones, kingdoms, rulers, and authorities" in this unseen realm. And the Bible doesn't stop there. We find countless references to angels, demons, and "rulers of the unseen world" throughout the Scriptures.

"There is another world, but it is in this one."

What is seen does not owe its existence to that which is visible. What is visible to our eyes is only a very small part of what science knows to exist. One of these days we may actually have instruments that can detect this other world, what we call the "spirit world" (Bolick, 2007).

Colossians 1:16 - "For by him were all things created, that are in heaven, and that are in earth, visible and invisible, whether they be thrones, or dominions, or principalities, or powers: all things were created by him, and for him" **(KJV)**.

There is another world that exists at this very moment on a parallel plane. It is invisible to the human eye, but just as real as the world we see. This invisible world influences everything that goes on in the earth. As a matter of fact, the earth itself was created from what we cannot see.

Hebrews 11:3 - "Through faith we understand that the worlds were framed by the word of God, so that things which are seen were not made of things which do appear" (**KJV**).

The Holy Spirit isn't all there is to the unseen. The Scriptures testify to the existence of other spirit-beings, such as angels and demons. They live in the unseen realms the ancients usually called 'heaven' and 'hell', which are more accurately described as being "in" or "out" of God's direct presence. Christianity does not demand that you believe in angels, demons, heaven or hell, especially not the way it's portrayed by popular culture. We could exchange comments endlessly about the many different interpretations of the Bible's portrayals of the supernatural. Yet, the Bible's authors are trying to describe the indescribable. At its core, Christianity is not really about the specific design of the world. It is about a relationship with God, and about God re-creating a single world where the unseen is finally free to be seen for what it really is. (Poets and songwriters instinctively know this.) God gave the Bible's many authors these insights and experiences to reveal real things about the different angles of a reality that right now includes both the seen and unseen.

The realities of the spiritual world are also often not visible to us humans, as the prophet Balaam discovered. He was trudging along the road with his two servants when his donkey "saw the Angel of the Lord standing in the way with His drawn sword in His hand."

Numbers 22:21-35 - "So Balaam rose in the morning, and saddled his ass, and went with the princes of Moab. But God's anger was kindled because he went; and the angel of the Lord took his stand in the way as his adversary. Now he was riding on the ass, and his two servants were with him. And the ass saw the angel of the Lord standing in the road, with a drawn sword in his hand; and the ass turned aside out of the road, and went into the field; and Balaam struck the ass, to turn her into the road. Then the angel of the LORD stood in a narrow path between the vineyards, with a wall on either side. And when the ass saw the angel of the LORD, she pushed against the wall, and pressed Balaam's foot against the wall; so he struck her again. Then the angel of the LORD went ahead, and stood in a narrow place, where there was no way to turn either to the right or to the left. When the ass saw the angel of the LORD, she lay down under Balaam; and Balaam's anger was kindled, and he struck the ass with his staff. Then the LORD opened the mouth of the ass, and she said to Balaam, "What have I done to you, that you have struck me these three times?" And Balaam said to the ass, "Because you have made sport of me. I wish I had a sword in my hand, for then I would kill you." And the ass said to Balaam, "Am I not your ass, upon which you have ridden all your life long to this day? Was I ever accustomed to do so to you?" And he said, "No." Then the LORD opened the eyes of Balaam, and he saw the angel of the LORD standing in the way, with his drawn sword in his hand; and he bowed his head, and fell on his face. And the angel of the LORD said to him, "Why have you struck your ass these three times? Behold, I have come forth to withstand you, because your way is perverse before me; and the ass saw me, and turned aside before me these three times. If she had not turned aside from me, surely just now I would have slain you and let her live." Then Balaam said to the angel of the LORD, "I have sinned, for I did not know that thou didst stand in the road against me. Now therefore, if it is evil in thy sight, I will go back again." And the angel of the LORD said to Balaam, "Go with the men; but only the word which I bid you, that shall you speak." So Balaam went on with the princes of Balak" (**RSV**).

To avoid the angel, the animal walked into a field, crushed Balaam's foot against a wall, and lay down with Balaam still on her back. Balaam was angry and struck the donkey. He didn't realize something supernatural was going on, until God opened his eyes in **verse 31**.

More than ever before, **"spiritual"** has become the word of choice for vague, foggy, and shrouded things with no rules, no substance, and really no definition. Anything that bears any amount of mystery is said to be spiritual. Some people even lump the paranormal in with it. To them, ghosts and magic and ESP and vampires are somehow part of spirituality. Web searches on 'spiritual' are less flaky but still cover a very wide range. The top ten include spiritual advisors, awakenings, poems, and healing. It's not just the world at large that loves using the term: many Christians speak way too glibly of spiritual gifts, and disciplines, disciplines, and worship, and fruit, and even *spiritual* warfare. They seek the spiritual meaning of words, but words don't work that way

To Christians, *spiritual,* refers to that which causes this world of stuff or material to come alive, to move, to change or resist change, or to take action (even when the action taken is to choose not to take action). The spiritual realm is supernatural, an aspect of what underlies all that happens in the material world, including ourselves, including everyone else around us. The material world is where the spiritual realm applies itself. This stuffy world is the meat and life-blood of the spiritual realm, and the spiritual is the life-force and thrust of the realm of substance. Thus, the two worlds are different angles of the same reality, not different or separate realities. The Kingdom that Jesus spoke of works in the same way: it came 2000 years ago when Jesus was born, it is here now through those who follow Him, and is coming in the future in its full form. The *spiritual* life (or soul-life) is lived in the material. And when it is completed, there will be no more mystery about how that can be.

One can be *spiritual* and not believe in Jesus as Christ. Such spirituality is to be treasured, and those who truly are that way are doing right by God. But it kind of misses the point: Christ was God's definitive act among humans. It's not that it does no good. It's a good beginning, it's just that without Christ, it has an incomplete or misdirected core to it. Spirituality, as important as it is, is not the key matter at hand; following Christ is the ANSWER! Sometimes, as Christians, we allow western thinking to affect our spiritual practices by attributing everything that happens in our lives to a natural cause and effect. The western worldview emphasizes that the only real things are what can be known or experienced through our five senses: hearing, seeing, smelling, tasting, and touching (Jacobs, 2015).

On the opposite end of the spectrum, there are those who want to blame every bad thing on demonic activity, often to the neglect of taking any personal responsibility for their own choices or actions. Giving in to either of these ways of thinking will cause failure and defeat. While it is true that some individuals can get absolutely strange in how they approach spiritual warfare, we should not fall into the trap of mocking biblical precedents, like the one given in (Jacobs, 2015):

Ephesian 6:12 - "For we wrestle not against flesh and blood, but against principalities, against powers, against the rulers of the darkness of this world, against spiritual wickedness in high places" (**KJV**).

There are times when every possible solution available in the natural will not change the outcome of a situation because our wrestling is not only with the physical realm, but also the unseen, spiritual realm. There are simply times in our lives when we try to do in the natural what can only be accomplished through the supernatural, but we can learn to recognize these moments and adjust our response. C. S. Lewis captured the importance of worldview when he offered this definition for the Christian worldview:

"I believe in Christianity as I believe that the sun has risen. Not only because I see it, but because by it I see everything else."

CHAPTER 2

HEAVENLY PLACES

As flesh-and-blood humans, we have very little understanding of the spirit world. We cannot see, hear, or touch it. However, the Bible assumes it, and we can glean insight into a world we cannot see by studying what God tells us about it. First of all:

- *God is spirit:*

John 4:24 - "God is spirit, and those who worship him must worship in spirit and truth" (**RSV**).

- *He exists outside the bounds of time, space, and matter. His home is called heaven:*

Acts 7:55 - "But he, full of the Holy Spirit, gazed into heaven and saw the glory of God, and Jesus standing at the right hand of God" (**RSV**).

Isaiah 63:15 - "Look down from heaven and see, from thy holy and glorious habitation. Where are thy zeal and thy might? The yearning of thy heart and thy compassion are withheld from me. But this is a distinct place, not to be confused with "the heavens," referring to the atmosphere" (**RSV**).

Genesis 1:1 - "In the beginning God created the heavens and the earth" (**RSV**).

Psalm 148:4 - "Praise him, you highest heavens, and you waters above the heavens" (**RSV**)!

Or the "heavenly realms," which encompass all spirit beings. In God's heaven, He sits on a throne.

Matthew 23:22 - "And he who swears by heaven, swears by the throne of God and by him who sits upon it" (**RSV**).

Hebrews 4:16 - "Let us then with confidence draw near to the throne of grace, that we may receive mercy and find grace to help in time of need" (**RSV**).

- *Surrounded by adoring angels:*

Revelation 7:11 - "And all the angels stood round the throne and round the elders and the four living creatures, and they fell on their faces before the throne and worshiped God" (**RSV**).

Psalm 99:1 - "The LORD reigns; let the peoples tremble! He sits enthroned upon the cherubim; let the earth quake! Who exist to serve God and minister to His saints" (**RSV**).

Hebrews 1:14 - "Are they not all ministering spirits sent forth to serve, for the sake of those who are to obtain salvation?" (**RSV**).

Matthew 4:11 - "Then the devil left him, and behold, angels came and ministered to him" (**RSV**).

Genesis 19:1 - "The two angels came to Sodom in the evening; and Lot was sitting in the gate of Sodom. When Lot saw them, he rose to meet them, and bowed himself with his face to the earth" (**RSV**).

- *Angels also have the ability to appear as men when sent to deliver messages from God:*

Genesis 18:2 - "He lifted up his eyes and looked, and behold, three men stood in front of him. When he saw them, he ran from the tent door to meet them, and bowed himself to the earth" (**RSV**).

Genesis 18:16-17 - "Then the men set out from there, and they looked toward Sodom; and Abraham went with them to set them on their way. The LORD said, "Shall I hide from Abraham what I am about to do" (**RSV**).

Genesis 19:1-2 - "The two angels came to Sodom in the evening; and Lot was sitting in the gate of Sodom. When Lot saw them, he rose to meet them, and bowed himself with his face to the earth, and said, 'My lords, turn aside, I pray you, to your servant's house and spend the night, and wash your feet; then you may rise up early and go on your way.' They said, 'No; we will spend the night in the street'" (**RSV**).

Daniel 10:5-6 - "I lifted up my eyes and looked, and behold, a man clothed in linen, whose loins were girded with gold of Uphaz. His body was like beryl, his face like the appearance of lightning, his eyes like flaming torches, his arms and legs like the gleam of burnished bronze, and the sound of his words like the noise of a multitude" (**RSV**).

One of the Scriptural words utilized in speaking of the unseen spiritual realm is a Greek word which is often translated heavenly or heavenly places. This word heavenly places speaks of a spiritual arena where explosive activity takes place, interactions and battles which affect our physical reality. We must remember, the unseen realm affects what occurs and takes place here in the seen realm of the earth.

However, the dark side of the heavenly realms belongs to Satan and his evil spirits. Satan is not the counterpart to God. God has no challenger. Satan is a created being who has only the power God allows him to have for only as long as God allows it:

Isaiah 14:12 - "How you have fallen from heaven, O star of the morning, son of the dawn! You have been cut down to the earth, You who have weakened the nations" (**NASB**).

Luke 22:31 - "Simon, Simon, behold, Satan has demanded *permission* to sift you like wheat;" (**NASB**).

Revelation 12:12 - "For this reason, rejoice, O heavens and you who dwell in them. Woe to the earth and the sea, because the devil has come down to you, having great wrath, knowing that he has *only* a short time" (**NASB**).

Yet, for reasons known only to God, Satan and his minions are allowed to wreak havoc upon the earth and the servants of God, if unchecked by spiritual warfare and the holy angels. **Daniel 10** gives us the best glimpse into what happens in this world we cannot see. An angel was dispatched by God to deliver a message to Daniel as he prayed, but the messenger was detained for three weeks by "the Prince of Persia", a demon (**verse 13**). The angel later told Daniel that he had to have help from Michael the archangel in order to prevail and continue on the assignment God had given him.

This glimpse into the heavenly realms helps us understand a few things. First, we learn that there is fierce warfare taking place at all times. Satan and his demons are actively working to thwart the plans of God and destroy whatever they can:

John 10:10 - "The thief comes only to steal and kill and destroy; I came that they may have life, and have *it* abundantly" (**NASB**).

If a mighty angel on a mission from God could be detained by demonic forces, then demons must have great power. Second, God does not leave His children defenseless against this evil army.

II Corinthians 10:4 - "For the weapons of our warfare are not of the flesh, but divinely powerful for the destruction of fortresses" (**NASB**).

Ephesians 6:11-17 - "Put on the full armor of God, so that you will be able to stand firm against the schemes of the devil. For our struggle is not against flesh and blood, but against the rulers, against the powers, against the world forces of this darkness, against the spiritual *forces* of wickedness in the heavenly *places*. Therefore, take up the full armor of God, so that you will be able to resist in the evil day, and having done everything, to stand firm. Stand firm therefore, HAVING GIRDED YOUR LOINS WITH TRUTH, and HAVING PUT ON THE BREASTPLATE OF RIGHTEOUSNESS, and having shod YOUR FEET WITH THE PREPARATION OF THE GOSPEL OF PEACE; in addition to all, taking up the shield of faith with which you will be able to extinguish all the flaming arrows of the evil *one*. And take THE HELMET OF SALVATION, and the sword of the Spirit, which is the word of God" (**NASB**).

This passage tells us exactly what armor we need to stand firm against the temptations and the schemes of the devil. In ourselves, we are no match for Satan's devices. We need spiritual armor to fight spiritual battles. The third truth we can learn from the Daniel passage is that prayer gets God's attention and that His answer is on the way. There are forces unknown to us that may interfere with God's desire to aid us, and we must continue to persevere in prayer until the answer comes:

Luke 18:1 - "Now He was telling them a parable to show that at all times they ought to pray and not to lose heart" (**NASB**).

Ephesians 6:18 - "With all prayer and petition pray at all times in the Spirit, and with this in view, be on the alert with all perseverance and petition for all the saints" (**NASB**).

The heavenly realms are as real as the earthly realms. We will spend most of our lives living in the heavenly realms:

II Corinthians 5:1 - "For we know that if the earthly tent which is our house is torn down, we have a building from God, a house not made with hands, eternal in the heavens" (**NASB**).

I John 5:11 - "And the testimony is this, that God has given us eternal life, and this life is in His Son" (**NASB**).

In contrast, our earthly existence is only a "vapor that appears for a little while and is gone":

James 4:14 - "Yet you do not know what your life will be like tomorrow. You are *just* a vapor that appears for a little while and then vanishes away" (**NASB**).

Physical battles may seem intense, but the results are temporary. However, spiritual battles have eternal consequences. When we live our earthly lives in recognition of the unseen battles that rage all around us, we will be more careful about what we say and do:

Ephesians 5:15-16 - "Therefore be careful how you walk, not as unwise men, but as wise, making the most of your time, because the days are evil" (**NASB**).

II Corinthians 2:11 - "So that no advantage would be taken of us by Satan, for we are not ignorant of his schemes" (**NASB**).

In the book of Ephesians, Paul uses *heavenly places* to give us a quick picture of the spiritual dimension, especially as it deals with believers and the corporate body of believers, the church. His prayer is that the eyes of our understanding, or in other words, our spiritual eyesight, would be opened to what is available and what is occurring in this invisible dimension.

- **Every spiritual blessing originates from God through Christ in the *heavenly places***

Ephesians 1:3 - "Blessed be the God and Father of our Lord Jesus Christ, who hath blessed us with all spiritual blessings in heavenly places in Christ:" (**KJV**).

Seeing this wording gives us a great deal of insight and encouragement. Heavenly places is a key dimension of the spirit realm, where Jesus Christ displays the victory of the cross through His church and where battles are fought over the thought patterns and decisions of mankind. With that in mind, I want to point out this phrase in the book of Ephesians to give you a vision of this unseen reality.

This awareness ought to open our eyes to the day to day battles you and I encounter. We must let the knowledge of God open our spiritual lenses so we can see what is at stake, that which stems from a dimension we cannot see with our five physical senses. Remember, only the Spirit can discern spiritual things. We need the Word of God to shed light where we have been operating in ignorance. Whether it is temptation, impressions, or imaginations that seem to appear as our own thoughts, we have an invisible enemy that is looking for agreement.

You can have the victory, but you must be aware of the WAR!

In perceiving the battleground of the *heavenly places*, the importance of recognizing our Source cannot be overlooked. We must first build the foundation that every available blessing originates from God in a spiritual dimension, or heavenly places. This means that my ability to experience love, joy, peace, victory and healing, to name some, has an origin from God in a spiritual realm.

As Christians, because of Christ, we have an opportunity to be God's children, and to see our heavenly Father as the source of all that we have access to. With this in mind, cultivating a grateful heart creates fertile soil for the God of heaven to do mighty things in our life. A thankful heart recognizes God as the giver of all good gifts. These gifts originate in an unseen realm and manifest in this physical reality. The more we recognize God as the source of all good things, it will also help us to learn how to cultivate a life in Christ that manifests continual blessings and overflow.

- **Jesus Christ is seated at the right hand of God in the *heavenly places.***

17

Ephesians 1:20-21 - "Which he wrought in Christ, when he raised him from the dead, and set him at his own right hand in the heavenly places, Far above all principality, and power, and might, and dominion, and every name that is named, not only in this world, but also in that which is to come:" **(KJV)**.

Because of what Christ accomplished through the cross and resurrection, He is now seated at the right hand of the Father, a place of dominion and ultimate authority. In the heavenly places, Christ is in His glorified state, possessing the keys of death and hell with power over all principalities and powers. All authority has been given to Him. His name is the name above all names. In fact, His name brings terror to all evil spirits in the heavenly places. They know who He is; they tremble before Him and are terrified by Him. With the name of Jesus, we have been given an authoritative name by which we can carry spiritual authority.

Jesus Christ, not only provided the way for eternal salvation, He showed us what the normal Christian life could be like for the body of Christ. God's desire is for the church as a whole to manifest Christ and the nature of Father God's heart here on earth. This was powerfully expressed through Jesus when He articulated that those who believe would actually do greater works than Himself. This means that in our lives, God's heart is for the sick to be healed, evil spirits to be removed, the broken restored, the dead raised and so much more in compounding measure. This is an amazing mandate given to God's children!

- **We as believers are seated with Christ in the *heavenly places*.**

Ephesians 2:6 - "And hath raised us up together, and made us sit together in heavenly places in Christ Jesus:" **(KJV)**.

Because of what Christ accomplished in His death and resurrection, there is a manifestation in the heavenly places of what this victory means for believers. God gives all those who believe in His Son the privilege of sitting with Christ. In the spiritual dimension, we have been given a place of authority, to receive and release the power that Christ paid.

This spiritual authority is a tremendous honor for believers. We can have authority over the powers of darkness! Yet our authority as Christians does not become applied without our cooperation and action. It must be activated in our lives through receiving the wisdom of God, having the mind of Christ and applying His powerful thinking in our lives. Part of the responsibility of sitting with Christ in heavenly places involves removing the enemy's way of thinking from our lives and putting it under our feet. When we do that, we make spiritual room for the thoughts and ways of God to fill us. Removing thought systems that do not line up with God's Word must be regularly applied in our lives so that true spiritual authority can manifest.

Spiritual authority truly becomes evident when Jesus, who is God the Word, becomes ingrained in our hearts. When His Word becomes implanted into our identity, then His identity has room to operate through us. When His identity is manifested in and through us, true spiritual authority can be activated. Additionally, the Holy Spirit works to confirm the Word in our lives. He takes that which we have hidden in our hearts and works to make it a part of our thinking so that it can be released with power in our lives (DeJesus, 2013).

Christ took authority and put all things under His feet in obedience to His assignment. As the head of the body of Christ, Jesus gave the church the opportunity to walk in that authority through obedience. Obedience involves taking God's Word and making it our way of thought in every aspect of our lives. Authority comes when we apply in our daily lives that which has been processed in our heart from God's Word. The way we are able to do this is by His Spirit's power.

Our divine calling is to display:
The wisdom of God to principalities and
powers in the *heavenly places*.

Ephesians 3:10 - "To the intent that now unto the principalities and powers in heavenly places might be known by the church the manifold wisdom of God" (**KJV**).

Part of our spiritual DNA involves all believers as one body, displaying the manifold wisdom of God in great splendor and power. *Wisdom* is a powerful way of thinking that has intelligence, creativity, clarity and council behind it. In this case, we are talking about the wisdom of God (DeJesus, 2013).

- **In the *heavenly places*, believers wrestle with Satan's army.**

Ephesians 6:12 - "For we wrestle not against flesh and blood, but against principalities, against powers, against the rulers of the darkness of this world, against spiritual wickedness in high places" (**KJV**).

Heavenly places are also a spiritual battleground where you and I wrestle against the powers of darkness. Our spiritual enemy seeks to prevent us from displaying God's wisdom (His magnificent way of thinking) in our lives. He does this through seeking to counterfeit and oppose God's thoughts in every way. Whether we choose to pay attention to this spiritual combat or not, the battle goes on nonetheless. While we sit in the heavenly places with Christ Jesus who won the victory, it is our responsibility to execute that victory and carry out that which Jesus paid for.

In Ephesians, Paul is teaching that although we walk in a physical existence, none of our battles are fought in that physical reality. Our battles are spiritual. They are spiritual battles that come down primarily to the exchange of thought, where we can receive and manifest God's way of thinking, or become deceived by agreeing with the enemy's subtle counterfeit thinking.

In Paul's letter to the Ephesian church regarding spiritual warfare, he taught them to engage by putting on the whole armor of God. Of course, this armor is God's armor, not our own. We must receive this armor and be taught in how to effectively use it. Each area of armament is intended to create a spiritual awareness to where we will be attacked and the tools that are available to defend as well as overcome and conquer. Understanding the armor of God helps us to be mindful of the attacks that stem from the invisible opposing kingdom and to guard our thinking against thought processes that go against the knowledge of God. Truth, righteousness, salvation and peace, which are all available to us in Christ Jesus, will be attacked and compromised at any opportunity.

If you have repented and trusted in Christ, then you are now, as I write this, seated with Christ, and "you are no longer strangers and aliens, but you are fellow citizens with the saints and members of the household of God" (**Ephesians 2:19, KJV**), and you are seated with fellow believers. How great is that!? Can we even fathom the idea that we are now, in God's mind, seated with Jesus Christ in heaven? Can we rest in that knowledge? If we rest in that, we can rest from trying to add works to our salvation because Jesus accomplished what we could not. He died so that we might live. That's what it means to be already seated with Christ in the heavenly places. Now you and I must seek out those who are still lost. We must find others to sit next to us who are already seated with Christ. For to do so will bring more glory to God and God is always pleased with us when we seek to glorify Him (Wellman, 2014).

CHAPTER 3

GATES OF HELL

T he idea of gates in the ancient world indicated a source of power. A small village may have only a simple entrance; a large, fortified city included a vast gate that could stand against a strong army. When Jesus made reference to the gates of hell, the most likely idea was an indication that all the power of hell and death could not overcome the power of the rock (Jesus Christ) to build the church (His called out assembly of people).

Matthew 16:15-18 - "He saith unto them, But whom say ye that I am? And Simon Peter answered and said, Thou art the Christ, the Son of the living God. And Jesus answered and said unto him, Blessed art thou, Simon Barjona: for flesh and blood hath not revealed it unto thee, but my Father which is in heaven. And I say also unto thee, That thou art Peter, and upon this rock I will build my church; and the gates of hell shall not prevail against it" (**KJV**).

Jesus said "I will build my church, and the gates of hell shall not prevail against it" but what was He talking about? Are there literal gates to hell that can be opened up and where the enemy can send forth wicked spirits against the church? In the first place, the word Jesus used for "hell" was "hades" or in this sentence, "the gates of Hades" so what is hades? The Bible uses different words for hell and sometimes it refers to sheol, hades, gehenna or the lake of fire."

The Greeks were certainly aware of what hades was from their writings of mythology and since the New Testament is almost entirely written in the Greek, we know that the Greek word "hades" refers to "Hades or Pluto, the god of the lower regions" which is the nether world or the realm of the dead but could also refer to the grave or death itself. Whichever of these uses are used, the meaning isn't changed; not even death or those of the "nether world" which could be demons or Satan will ever prevail against, stop or prevent the church from surviving (Wellman, Jack, 2014).

The last part of the verse Jesus said that "the gates of hell shall not prevail against it" is the word for "prevail" being the Greek word and this means "to be superior too" or "to overcome" so clearly nothing and no one (man, Satan, or his demons) can ever overcome Jesus' church. That doesn't mean that Satan won't persecute the church and this means the individual members of the church as we will later read in the Book of Revelation. Satan has so self-deluded himself that he actually thinks he can take down the church but of course he cannot possibly do this. He can hurt the church, divide the church, and cause her great harm, but in the end, he cannot destroy the church. This seems strange because Satan is well versed in the Bible and he must know that his fate is sealed and that the Bible is clear that he will never take down the church but sometimes rage has a way of clouding reason, logic, and rational thought (Wellman, Jack, 2014).

When we read "hell," we naturally think of the realm of the unbelieving dead. But the Greek word translated "hell", is also the name for the Underworld, the realm of *all* the dead, not just unbelievers. The Hebrew equivalent to *hades* is Sheol, the place "under the earth," where all went after this life ended. While the imagery associated with the Underworld would have unnerved the disciples, Jesus' reference to the gates of *hades* would have jolted them for another reason. If they knew their Old Testament well, they understood that they were standing before those very gates as Jesus spoke.

Matthew 16 takes place in Caesarea Philippi, situated near a mountainous region containing Mount Hermon. In the Old Testament, this region was known as Bashan, a place with a sinister reputation. According to the Old Testament, Bashan was controlled by two kings, Sihon and Og, who were associated with the ancient giant clans: the Rephaim and the Anakim.

Deuteronomy 2:10-12 - "The Emims dwelt therein in times past, a people great, and many, and tall, as the Anakims; Which also were accounted giants, as the Anakims; but the Moabites called them Emims. The Horims also dwelt in Seir beforetime; but the children of Esau succeeded them, when they had destroyed them from before them, and dwelt in their stead; as Israel did unto the land of his possession, which the LORD gave unto them" (**KJV**).

Joshua 12:1–5 - "Now these are the kings of the land, which the children of Israel smote, and possessed their land on the other side Jordan toward the rising of the sun, from the river Arnon unto mount Hermon, and all the plain on the east: Sihon king of the Amorites, who dwelt in Heshbon, and ruled from Aroer, which is upon the bank of the river Arnon, and from the middle of the river, and from half Gilead, even unto the river Jabbok, which is the border of the children of Ammon; And from the plain to the sea of Chinneroth on the east, and unto the sea of the plain, even the salt sea on the east, the way to Bethjeshimoth; and from the south, under Ashdothpisgah: And the coast of Og king of Bashan, which was of the remnant of the giants, that dwelt at Ashtaroth and at Edrei, And reigned in mount Hermon, and in Salcah, and in all Bashan, unto the border of the Geshurites and the Maachathites, and half Gilead, the border of Sihon king of Heshbon" (**KJV**).

The two main cities of their kingdom were Ashtaroth and Edrei, home to the Rephaim:

Deuteronomy 3:1 - "Then we turned, and went up the way to Bashan: and Og the king of Bashan came out against us, he and all his people, to battle at Edrei" (**KJV**).

Deuteronomy 3:10–11 - "All the cities of the plain, and all Gilead, and all Bashan, unto Salchah and Edrei, cities of the kingdom of Og in Bashan. For only Og king of Bashan remained of the remnant of giants; behold his bedstead was a bedstead of iron; is it not in Rabbath of the children of Ammon? Nine cubits was the length thereof, and four cubits the breadth of it, after the cubit of a man" (**KJV**).

Joshua 12:4–5 - "And the coast of Og king of Bashan, which was of the remnant of the giants, that dwelt at Ashtaroth and at Edrei, And reigned in mount Hermon, and in Salcah, and in all Bashan, unto the border of the Geshurites and the Maachathites, and half Gilead, the border of Sihon king of Heshbon" (**KJV**).

To make the region even more unique, Caesarea Philippi had been built and dedicated to Zeus. This pagan god was worshipped at a religious center built a short distance from the more ancient one in Daat the foot of Mount Hermon. Aside from the brief interlude during the time of Joshua through Solomon, the gates of hell were continually open for business. It is the Church that Jesus sees as the aggressor. He was declaring war on evil and death. Jesus would build His Church atop the gates of hell; He would bury them.

When Satan (the dragon) tried to destroy Jesus as a baby, he failed as His parents fled to Egypt for safety:

Revelation 12:1-6 - "A great sign appeared in heaven: a woman clothed with the sun, with the moon under her feet and a crown of twelve stars on her head. She was pregnant and cried out in pain as she was about to give birth. Then another sign appeared in heaven: an enormous red dragon with seven heads and ten horns and seven crowns on its heads. Its tail swept a third of the stars out of the sky and flung them to the earth. The dragon stood in front of the woman who was about to give birth, so that it might devour her child the moment he was born. She gave birth to a son, a male child, who "will rule all the nations with an iron scepter." And her child was snatched up to God and to his throne. The woman fled into the wilderness to a place prepared for her by God, where she might be taken care of for 1,260 days" (**NIV**).

And after war broke out in heaven, Satan couldn't prevail against Michael and his angels:

Revelation 12:7-9 - "Then war broke out in heaven. Michael and his angels fought against the dragon, and the dragon and his angels fought back. But he was not strong enough, and they lost their place in heaven. The great dragon was hurled down, that ancient serpent called the devil, or Satan, who leads the whole world astray. He was hurled to the earth, and his angels with him" (**NIV**).

And he was so enraged by this that "the dragon became furious with the woman and went off to make war on the rest of her offspring, on those who keep the commandments of God and hold to the testimony of Jesus:"

Revelation 12:17 - "Then the dragon was enraged at the woman and went off to wage war against the rest of her offspring, those who keep God's commands and hold fast their testimony about Jesus" (**NIV**).

And that is most certainly Jesus' church for who else keeps the commands of God and holds to the testimony of Jesus?

"Her offspring" is the very church that Jesus built and which He said the gates of hell couldn't prevail or overthrow it. Later we read that "it was allowed to make war on the saints and to conquer them. And authority was given it over every tribe and people and language and nation, and all who dwell on earth will worship it, everyone whose name has not been written before the foundation of the world in the book of life of the Lamb who was slain."

Revelation 13:7-8 - "It was given power to wage war against God's holy people and to conquer them. And it was given authority over every tribe, people, language and nation. All inhabitants of the earth will worship the beast—all whose names have not been written in the Lamb's book of life, the Lamb who was slain from the creation of the world" (**NIV**).

But these verses never say that the church is destroyed. Many martyrs have and yet will lose their life for their faith but that never prevails against their entering the kingdom (Wellman, Jack, 2014). The phrase the "gates of hell" is translated in some versions as the "gates of Hades." "Gates of hell" or "gates of Hades" is found only once in the entire Scriptures in:

Matthew 16:18 - "And I tell you that you are Peter. On this rock I will build My church. The powers of hell will not be able to have power over My church" (**NIV**).

Also, in this passage, Jesus is referring to the building of His church. At that time Jesus had not yet established His church. In fact, this is the first instance of the word *church* in the New Testament. The word *church*, as used by Jesus, is derived from the Greek *ekklasia*, which means the "called out" or "assembly." In other words, the church that Jesus is referencing as His church is the assembly of people who have been called out of the world by the gospel of Christ.

Bible scholars debate the actual meaning of the phrase "and the gates of hell shall not prevail against it." One of the better interpretations to the meaning of this phrase is as follows. In ancient times, the cities were surrounded by walls with gates, and in battles the gates of these cities would usually be the first place their enemies assaulted. This was because the protection of the city was determined by the strength or power of its gates (Wellman, Jack, 2014).

Jesus refers here to His impending death. Though He would be crucified and buried, He would rise from the dead and build His church. Jesus is emphasizing the fact that the powers of death could not hold Him in. Not only would the church be established in spite of the powers of Hades or hell, but the church would thrive in spite of these powers. The church will never fail, though generation after generation succumbs to the power of physical death, yet other generations will arise to perpetuate the church. And it will continue until it has fulfilled its mission on earth as Jesus has commanded:

Matthew 28:18-20 - "All authority in heaven and on earth has been given to me. Go therefore and make disciples of all nations, baptizing them in the name of the Father and of the Son and of the Holy Spirit, teaching them to observe all that I have commanded you. And behold, I am with you always, to the end of the age" (**ESV**).

It is clear that Jesus was declaring that death has no power to hold God's people captive. Its gates are not strong enough to overpower and keep imprisoned the church of God. The Lord has conquered death:

Romans 8:2 - "Because through Christ Jesus the law of the Spirit who gives life has set you free from the law of sin and death" (**NIV**).

Acts 2:24 - "But God raised him from the dead, freeing him from the agony of death, because it was impossible for death to keep its hold on him" (**NIV**).

And because "death no longer is master over Him":

Romans 6:9 - "For we know that since Christ was raised from the dead, he cannot die again; death no longer has mastery over him" (**NIV**).

Even today Satan has his own ministers behind the pulpits of many churches and you can tell who they are by what they don't preach like on repentance, the blood the Lamb, the cross, the forgiveness of sins, and the security of trusting in Christ. This shouldn't surprise us for it is "no wonder, for even Satan disguises himself as an angel of light."

II Corinthians 11:14 - "And no wonder, for Satan himself masquerades as an angel of light" (**NIV**).

Satan is a liar and has been from the beginning:

John 8:44 - "You belong to your father, the devil, and you want to carry out your father's desires. He was a murderer from the beginning, not holding to the truth, for there is no truth in him. When he lies, he speaks his native language, for he is a liar and the father of lies" (**NIV**).

But the truth of God will prevail just as the church will. Paul warned that "the Spirit expressly says that in later times some will depart from the faith by devoting themselves to deceitful spirits and teachings of demons, through the insincerity of liars whose consciences are seared."

I Timothy 4:1-2 - "The Spirit clearly says that in later times some will abandon the faith and follow deceiving spirits and things taught by demons. Such teachings come through hypocritical liars, whose consciences have been seared as with a hot iron" (**NIV**).

Conclusion

We know that the gates of death or hell nor anything or anyone else will prevail against the Church for Jesus is the Head of the Church and He prevails over all that He has created. The Church is no exception and so we can rest assured that not even the gates of hell will ever prevail against the Church. That means that even death itself cannot prevail against the saints of God because their destiny is as secure as the eternalness of Jesus and all of His precious promises are yes and amen. So preach and believe in:

Matthew 16:18 - "And I tell you that you are Peter, and on this rock I will build my church, and the gates of Hades will not overcome it" (**NIV**).

But don't misunderstand the promise. Jesus assures us of something better than world transformation. He promises eternal life. Truly, with intense opposition and persecution, the early church was under at tack from the gates of hell. But just as Jesus conquered the grave, so the gates of hell, death itself, will not prevail against those who belong to Christ. As Jesus Himself put it, "Whoever believes in me, though he die, yet shall he live."

John 11:25 - "Jesus said to her, "I am the resurrection and the life. The one who believes in me will live, even though they die" (**NIV**).

Indeed, the Church that endures to the end, the Church that frees the living from the power of sin and death is also the Church that prevails against whatever trials and temptations the devil and the other demonic powers of hell bring against it. Put simply, the gates of hell no longer can keep the people of God, the true members of His Church, out of heaven. What a wonderful promise this truly is!

I am the resurrection and the life.

CHAPTER 4

AN UNSEEN STRUGGLE ... LIFE ITSELF

W e Christians live right in the midst of the world. That is where we are supposed to be. We recognize that as Christians we live in the world, but don't assume that because we are living here we must be like the world. We don't have to think like the world, nor do we have to depend upon the thoughts, philosophies, ideas, and writers of the world, and draw all our arguments and our solutions to problems from these sources. This is not how a Christian should approach these problems. As the Apostle Paul put it in this this letter:

II Corinthians 4:18 - "Because we look not to the things that are seen but to the things that are unseen; for the things that are seen are transient, but the things that are unseen are eternal" (**RSV**).

There is a new dimension that must come in here. The Christian approach to any basic problem, whether of society or in an individual life, must be different than that of the world if we expect solutions for our problems. The wonderful thing about the scriptures is that life is constantly confirming them. If we observe enough of life over a long enough span, which is right and which is wrong, the worldly solution, or the scriptural solution, scriptural principles work out for us.

In this world we experience struggles; we may encounter times of poverty, sickness, and persecution. The world often labels us as worthless. But the truth is that in Christ, we are healed and loved. We are royalty and co-heirs with Christ. What is "unseen" about us as children of God is truer than the "seen" we experience in this life. We fix our eyes on the unseen truth. We live our lives based on the unseen rather than the seen (Howard, 2016).

God's Word promises us peace, joy, strength, healing, rest, victory, eternal life, and many other promises too numerous to list! These promises aren't limited to the future. They are for now. They are for this life. We are a nation of royal priests, co-heirs with Christ, and the light of the world. The Bible says we are, not we will be (Howard, 2016).

It is God's desire for His children to live by the truth of the unseen rather than the lies of the seen.

Reality is not what we can see, rather it is in what we can't see. Reality is God. It's His Son. It's the Holy Spirit living within us allowing us to worship the Father in spirit and in truth. The spiritual realm is far more real than the physical realm. We may not understand it fully now, but we will. The physical will pass away, but the unseen will last forever (Howard, 2016).

II Corinthians 4:17-18 - "For our light affliction, which is but for a moment, worketh for us a far more exceeding and eternal weight of glory; While we look not at the things which are seen, but at the things which are not seen: for the things which are seen are temporal; but the things which are not seen are eternal" (**KJV**).

Anyone who reads the New Testament sees that this is always the way of the world. Its solutions are fundamentally shallow and superficial, because they are essentially one-dimensional. Their approach lacks something and it is because it is one-dimensional. All of us face problems, normal, common problems, depression, discouragement, ill health, lack of money, social pressures, family troubles, in-laws, greed, guilt, shame. As a society, we face problems together, race tensions, war, poverty, air and water pollution, inflation, death, taxes, all these common problems.

When you are sick and in need of healing...
When you're facing a crisis you can't handle on your own...
When you're overcome with grief or sadness...
When you are overwhelmed and overworked...
When you're struggling with circumstances beyond your control...
Trust the unseen

Satan wants nothing more than to enter certain areas of your life so he can gain a stronghold. He'll try anything to throw you off center, distract you from your focus, and render you ineffective for the Kingdom of God.

Notice: This portion of my chapter was written by Cindi McMenamin. The name of the article is: *"5 Areas of Your Life Satan Wants to Enter"* written in the publication Crosswalk.

These are the five areas of your life Satan wants to enter:

- **Your heart ... so it's not God's alone.**

There's a reason God's Word tells us:

Proverbs 4:23 - "Above all else, guard your heart, for everything you do flows from it" (**NIV**).

Satan knows he has an entry point into your life if God is not first in our hearts. God's first commandment, set forth under the Old Covenant was:

Exodus 20:3 - "You shall have no other gods before me" (**NIV**).

And Jesus restated that under the New Covenant when He was asked what is the greatest commandment and responded by saying:

Luke 10:27 - "Love the Lord your God with all your heart and with all your soul and with all your strength and with all your mind ..." (**NIV**).

Satan's greatest desire is to prevent you from giving God *all* of your heart so he will constantly dangle people, things, and desires in front of you, anything to distract you so he can erect a false god in front of you that you don't even realize you have.

Do you love God more than you love anything (or anyone) else in life?

He will try to lure you with a false god like your career, a spouse or love interest, a dream or goal, a hobby or lifestyle. I know many women whose first love is their bodies, so they spend more time in the gym working out than letting God work within. It's a subtle way of starting to love other things more than God. Some of us love food, money, recreation, our children, a substance, or a "feeling" (like being in love, or feeling energetic) more than God, Himself. Guard your heart by keeping Christ on the throne of your life so Satan doesn't try to sneak anything else in there.

- **Your worries ... to make you doubt God's love and provision.**

Satan wants you stressing, because then you're not resting in God's ability to care for you. Women tend to stress over the temporal, bills that must be paid, whether or not a man will come into our lives, if we'll be able to have a child, what someone is saying about us, how our body looks, and so on. Men tend to stress about their jobs, providing for their families, and whether or not they are "making the cut" in several areas of life. Then there's health concerns, fears about our aging parents, and other situations that can crowd out God's peace in our lives and even cause us to begin to blame God for our circumstances.

Are you living like God's love and provision are real?

Don't let Satan in this door through his tantalizing "what if?" questions and the doubts he weaves through your mind. God instructs us in:

Philippians 4:6-7 - "Be anxious for nothing, but in everything by prayer and supplication with thanksgiving let your requests be made known to God. And the peace of God, which surpasses all comprehension, will guard your hearts and your minds in Christ Jesus" (**NASB**).

Keep praying about your concerns and keep thanking God ahead of time for what He's about to do, so Satan doesn't get a stronghold in your mind through your worries and fears.

- **Your everyday thinking ... so you're just like the world**

It's amazing how many people profess to know God and follow Him, yet their thinking patterns are just like those of anyone else in the world. Satan loves that. He wants you to be so absorbed with the ways of the world that you are clueless about what God's Word says. He will do this through subtle messages in music lyrics, statements from your favorite celebrity, and words of advice from friends, even friends of yours who are believers, but are quoting "verses" that are not in the Bible.

Is your everyday thinking different from the world's?

Scripture commands us:

Romans 12:2 - "Don't copy the behavior and customs of this world, but let God transform you into a new person by changing the way you think. Then you will know what God wants you to do, and you will know how good and pleasing and perfect his will really is" (**NLT**).

Furthermore, God's Word instructs:

Philippians 4:8-9 - "Fix your thoughts on what is true and honorable and right. Think about things that are pure and lovely and admirable. Think about things that are excellent and worthy of praise… and the God of peace will be with you" (**NLT**).

But Satan would rather have us in mental anguish by listening to the world, rather than the word of God. Guard your everyday thinking by soaking it in Scripture. It's the only way to keep Satan and his worldly philosophies from entering in.

- **Your speech … so you tear others apart.**

God wants us to be holy mouthpieces for Him, people who heal and help with our words. But Satan would rather have you and me blowing it big time with our mouths. A few critical words here, a few complaints there, some profanity mixed in with a little gossip on the side and we have given him permission to make us people who tear others apart and sound no different (and sometimes worse) than unbelievers. Satan knows we can cause much damage with our mouths if we do not bring them under God's control.

Are your words building up others?

Whether it is gossip, criticism or unkind remarks, our mouths can be instruments of righteousness or unrighteousness. Close that door to Satan, altogether, by applying God's instructions in:

Ephesians 4:29 - "Do not let any unwholesome talk come out of your mouths, but only what is helpful for building others up according to their needs, that it may benefit those who listen" (**NIV**).

And **I Thessalonians 5:18** tells us - "In everything give thanks; for this is God's will for you in Christ Jesus" (**NASB**).

Be a verbally thankful person who speaks only to lift others up, not tear them down. That will diminish and destroy a critical and complaining spirit that gives Satan a stronghold in our lives.

- **Our Bodies ... so they no longer glorify God.**

Why is it that when people get depressed they overeat or drink excessively or turn to substances? Why is it that young girls will cut their bodies or starve themselves when they are dealing with emotional pain? I believe it's because Satan will turn us against our bodies if he can, as a way of "getting back at God." Our bodies are precious to God. Scripture commands us to

Romans 12:1 - "Give your bodies to God. Let them be a living and holy sacrifice – the kind he will accept. When you think of what he has done for you, is this too much to ask?" (**NLT**).

Are you glorifying God through your body?

Satan knows that God considers our bodies His temple and therefore God wants us to keep our bodies holy, healthy and honoring to Him:

I Corinthians 6:19-20 - "Do you not know that your bodies are temples of the Holy Spirit, who is in you, whom you have received from God? You are not your own; you were bought at a price. Therefore honor God with your bodies" (**NIV**).

Romans 12:1 - "Therefore, I urge you, brothers and sisters, in view of God's mercy, to offer your bodies as a living sacrifice, holy and pleasing to God, this is your true and proper worship" (**NIV**).

So because our bodies are holy to God, Satan would love to have us harm them, mutilate them, starve them, and destroy them with substances. Don't let him in. Not in how you dress. Not in how you see yourself. Not in how you treat yourself. Ask God for a healthy body image and a desire to protect your body so you can serve Him on this earth in it for as long as possible. So what's your strategy now that you know the areas where Satan wants to enter your life? God gives us a great defense through

Paul's instructions to the saints in:

Ephesians 6:11-18 - "Put on the full armor of God, so that you can take your stand against the devil's schemes. For our struggle is not against flesh and blood, but against the rulers, against the authorities, against the powers of this dark world and against the spiritual forces of evil in the heavenly realms. Therefore put on the full armor of God, so that when the day of evil comes, you may be able to stand your ground, and after you have done everything, to stand. Stand firm then, with the belt of truth buckled around your waist, with the breastplate of righteousness in place, and with your feet fitted with the readiness that comes from the gospel of peace. In addition to all this, take up the shield of faith, with which you can extinguish all the flaming arrows of the evil one. Take the helmet of salvation and the sword of the Spirit, which is the word of God. And pray in the Spirit on all occasions with all kinds of prayers and requests. With this in mind, be alert and always keep on praying for all the Lord's people" (**NIV**).

The best way to handle the *"STRUGGLES of LIFE"* is to bring them to the Lord. I often want to fix my problems by myself, but need to remind myself that God is loving and all powerful and wants to help me get through life's struggles. God's word can aid in taking your worries away and has clear instructions on how to bring your problems to the Lord! Isn't that amazing?

Here are 10 bible verses you can refer to when you are faced with difficulties and stress!

1. **Psalm 46:1-2, 7** - "God is our refuge and strength, an ever-present help in trouble. Therefore, we will not fear, though the earth give way and the mountains fall into the heart of the sea; The Lord Almighty is with us; the God of Jacob is our fortress" (**NIV**).

2. **Isaiah 12:2** - "Surely God is my salvation; I will trust and not be afraid. The Lord, the Lord himself, is my strength and my defense."

3. **Matthew 6:34** - "Therefore do not worry about tomorrow, for tomorrow will worry about itself. Each day has enough trouble of its own."

4. **Jeremiah 17:7** - "But blessed is the one who trusts in the Lord, whose confidence is in him."

5. **Philippians 4:6** - "Do not be anxious about anything, but in every situation, by prayer and petition, with thanksgiving, present your requests to God."

6. **1 Peter 5:6-7** - "Humble yourselves, therefore, under God's mighty hand, that he may lift you up in due time. Cast all your anxiety on him because he cares for you."

7. **John 14:27** - "Peace I leave with you; my peace I give you. I do not give to you as the world gives. Do not let your hearts be troubled and do not be afraid."

8. **Psalm 55:22** - "Cast your cares on the Lord and he will sustain you; he will never let the righteous be shaken."

9. **Psalm 23:4** - "Even though I walk through the darkest valley, I will fear no evil, for you are with me; your rod and your staff they comfort me."

10. **Jeremiah 29:11** - "For I know the plans I have for you," declares the Lord, "plans to prosper you and not to harm you, plans to give you hope and a future."

I hope that these bible verses will be able to bring you some peace and relief in the future. Just remind yourself that God is your strength and your refuge and to lay your struggles before Him! He loves you immensely and wants to lighten your load (heart and your mind). In the future, when you're faced with stress and struggles, try referencing these wonderful verses! They are sure to help you feel a million times better!

Bring your "STRUGGLES of LIFE" to the Lord!

CHAPTER 5

UNSEEN SPIRITUAL BEINGS

I f you've ever been puzzled about angels, demons, and other spiritual beings in the Bible, you're not alone! Our modern depictions of these creatures are mostly based on misunderstandings of who they are and how they fit into the overall story line of the Bible. In the opening pages of the Bible, God creates two overlapping realms, the heavens and the earth. This is where the drama of the biblical story line takes place. Many of us are familiar with the earthly drama. Humans are given a wonderful garden to rule on God's behalf, but they lose access to this paradise because of a foolish rebellion.

But the biblical authors want us to see another set of characters, the inhabitants of the heavenly realm who are also heavily involved in this earthly story. The Bible tells us that there are many spirit persons. God is himself a spirit:

John 4:24 - "For God is Spirit, so those who worship him must worship in spirit and in truth" (**NLT**).

II Corinthians 3:17-18 - "For the Lord is the Spirit, and wherever the Spirit of the Lord is, there is freedom. So all of us who have had that veil removed can see and reflect the glory of the Lord. And the Lord, who is the Spirit, makes us more and more like him as we are changed into his glorious image" (**NLT**).

At one time God was alone in the universe. Then he began to create spirit persons called angels. They are more powerful and more intelligent than humans. Jehovah created many angels; God's servant Daniel, in a vision, saw a hundred million angels" (**NLT**).

Daniel 7:10 - "And a river of fire was pouring out, flowing from his presence. Millions of angels ministered to him; many millions stood to attend him. Then the court began its session, and the books were opened" (**NLT**).

Hebrews 1:7 - "Regarding the angels, he says, 'He sends his angels like the winds, his servants like flames of fire'" (**NLT**).

These angels were created by God even before he made the earth.

Job 38:4-7 - "Where were you when I laid the foundations of the earth? Tell me, if you know so much" (**NLT**).

Who determined its dimensions and stretched out the surveying line? What supports its foundations, and who laid its cornerstone as the morning stars sang together and all the angels shouted for joy? None of them are people who once lived and died on earth. The Bible refers to angels hundreds of times. Let us consider a few of these references to learn more about angels. Where did angels come from?

Colossians 1:16 says: "For through him God created everything in the heavenly realms and on earth. He made the things we can see and the things we can't see, such as thrones, kingdoms, rulers, and authorities in the unseen world. Everything was created through him and for him. All the spirit creatures called angels were individually created by Jehovah God through his firstborn Son. How many angels are there? The Bible indicates that hundreds of millions of angels were created, and all of them are powerful" (**NLT**).

Psalm 103:20 - "Praise the LORD, you angels, you mighty ones who carry out his plans, listening for each of his commands" (**NLT**).

Ever since they witnessed the creation of the first humans, faithful spirit creatures have shown keen interest in the growing human family and in the outworking of God's purpose.

Proverbs 8:30-31 - "I was the architect at his side. I was his constant delight, rejoicing always in his presence. And how happy I was with the world he created; how I rejoiced with the human family" (**NLT**)!

I Peter 1:11-12 - "They wondered what time or situation the Spirit of Christ within them was talking about when he told them in advance about Christ's suffering and his great glory afterward. They were told that their messages were not for themselves, but for you. And now this Good News has been announced to you by those who preached in the power of the Holy Spirit sent from heaven. It is all so wonderful that even the angels are eagerly watching these things happen" (**NLT**).

With the passing of time, however, the angels observed that most of the human family turned away from serving their loving Creator. No doubt this saddened the faithful angels. On the other hand, whenever even one human returns to Jehovah, "joy arises among the angels."

Luke 15:10 - "In the same way, there is joy in the presence of God's angels when even one sinner repents" (**NLT**).

Since angels have such deep concern for the welfare of those who serve God, it is no wonder that God has repeated used angels to strengthen and protect his faithful servants on earth. Today, angels no longer appear visibly to God's people on earth. Although invisible to human eyes, God's powerful angels still protect his people, especially from anything spiritually harmful. The Bible says: "The angel of Jehovah camps all around those fearing Him, and he rescues them."

Psalm 34:7 - "For the angel of the LORD is a guard; he surrounds and defends all who fear him" (**NLT**).

Why should those words be of great comfort to us? Because there are dangerous, wicked spirit creatures who want to destroy us! Who are they? Where do they come from? How are they trying to harm us? To find out, let us briefly consider something that happened at the start of human history.

As stated in **Genesis Chapter 3** of the Bible, one of the angels developed a desire to rule over others and thus turned against God. Later this angel became known as Satan the Devil.

Revelation 12:9 - "This great dragon, the ancient serpent called the devil, or Satan, the one deceiving the whole world, was thrown down to the earth with all his angels" (**NLT**).

During the 16 centuries after he deceived Eve, Satan succeeded in turning away from God nearly all humans except a few faithful ones, such as Abel, Enoch, and Noah:

Hebrews 11:4-7 - "It was by faith that Abel brought a more acceptable offering to God than Cain did. Abel's offering gave evidence that he was a righteous man, and God showed his approval of his gifts. Although Abel is long dead, he still speaks to us by his example of faith. It was by faith that Enoch was taken up to heaven without dying, 'he disappeared, because God took him.' For before he was taken up, he was known as a person who pleased God. And it is impossible to please God without faith. Anyone who wants to come to him must believe that God exists and that he rewards those who sincerely seek him. It was by faith that Noah built a large boat to save his family from the flood. He obeyed God, who warned him about things that had never happened before. By his faith

Noah condemned the rest of the world, and he received the righteousness that comes by faith" (**NLT**).

The disobedient angels exercise a very bad influence over humans. In fact, with the help of these demons, Satan "is misleading the entire inhabited earth":

Revelation 12:9 - "This great dragon, the ancient serpent called the devil, or Satan, the one deceiving the whole world, was thrown down to the earth with all his angels" (**NLT**).

I John 5:19 - "We know that we are children of God and that the world around us is under the control of the evil one" (**NLT**).

How? Mainly, the demons use methods designed to mislead people. Wicked spirits not only mislead people but also frighten them. Today, Satan and his demons know that they have only "a short period of time" left before they are put out of action, and they are now more vicious than ever.

Revelation 12:12 - "Therefore, rejoice, O heavens! And you who live in the heavens, rejoice! But terror will come on the earth and the sea, for the devil has come down to you in great anger, knowing that he has little time" (**NLT**).

Revelation 12:17 - "And the dragon was angry at the woman and declared war against the rest of her children, all who keep God's commandments and maintain their testimony for Jesus" (**NLT**).

Even so, thousands of people who once lived in daily dread of such wicked spirits have been able to break free. How did they do this? Wicked spirits are dangerous, but we need not live in fear of them if we oppose the Devil and draw close to God by doing His will.

James 4:7-8 - "So humble yourselves before God. Resist the devil, and he will flee from you. 8 Come close to God, and God will come close to you. Wash your hands, you sinners; purify your hearts, for your loyalty is divided between God and the world" (**NLT**).

The power of the wicked spirits is limited. They were punished in Noah's day, and they face their final judgment in the future.

Jude 6 - "And I remind you of the angels who did not stay within the limits of authority God gave them but left the place where they belonged. God has kept them securely chained in prisons of darkness, waiting for the great day of judgment" (**NLT**).

Remember, too, that we have the protection of God's powerful angels.

II Kings 6:15-17 - "When the servant of the man of God got up early the next morning and went outside, there were troops, horses, and chariots everywhere. 'Oh, sir, what will we do now?' The young man cried to Elisha. 'Don't be afraid!' Elisha told him. 'For there are more on our side than on theirs!' Then Elisha prayed, 'O Lord, open his eyes and let him see!' The Lord opened the young man's eyes, and when he looked up, he saw that the hillside around Elisha was filled with horses and chariots of fire" (**NLT**).

Those angels are deeply interested in seeing us succeed in resisting wicked spirits. The righteous angels are cheering us on, so to speak. Let us therefore stay close to Jehovah and his family of faithful spirit creatures. May we also avoid every kind of spiritism and always apply the counsel of God's Word.

I Peter 5:6-7 - "So humble yourselves under the mighty power of God, and at the right time he will lift you up in honor. Give all your worries and cares to God, for he cares about you" (**NLT**).

II Peter 2:9 - "So you see, the Lord knows how to rescue godly people from their trials, even while keeping the wicked under punishment until the day of final judgment" (**NLT**).

We can be sure of victory in our fight!

CHAPTER 6

THE INVISIBLE WAR

W hether we know it or not, all Christians are engaged in a titanic spiritual battle, not against the forces of any earthly nation, but against the forces of darkness. This war is between good and bad, between righteousness and evil, between truth and falsehood. God is the source of all good, and with Him are good angels and His people. The initiator of evil is Satan, and he is allied with demons and all those whom Satan can deceive into serving his purposes.

God's purpose is to fill all of creation with His glory. So He works to advance righteousness, goodness, peace, love and joy, and to call people to believe in Him and become citizens of heaven even while they live on earth. Satan's purpose is to spoil all of creation and to deny and oppose God's glory how- ever he can, so Satan advances sin, evil, hatred, and despair, and seeks to prevent people from believing in God and be-coming citizens of heaven. God's strategy is to enlighten and save. Satan's strategy is to deceive and destroy (Koukl, 2017).

This Battle is Largely Unseen . . . An Invisible War.

Spiritual warfare occurs in our everyday lives in different ways, sometimes blatantly, but often very subtly. Things go on behind the scenes that we do not naturally perceive or understand. Yet these invisible acts and forces often determine spiritual victories or defeats. We must understand spiritual warfare if we are to emerge spiritually victorious.

Ephesians 6:10-12 - "Finally, be strong in the Lord and in his mighty power. Put on the full armor of God, so that you can take your stand against the devil's schemes. For our struggle is not against flesh and blood, but against the rulers, against the authorities, against the powers of this dark world and against the spiritual forces of evil in the heavenly realms" (**NIV**).

Paul clearly states that we are called to fight a spiritual battle against the rulers, authorities, the powers of the dark world, and spiritual forces of evil. We are called to engage in spiritual warfare. But, what is spiritual warfare? The enemy's attacks are always wrapped in the packaging of deception, always designed to manipulate the truth about God, and about your value in Him. He desires to lead you into sin so that fellowship is broken between you and God, this way you'll be disconnected from the Source of true power and strength (Shirer, 2016).

The evil temptations that appeal to your specific desires and happen to show up when you are most vulnerable are not accidental. We're in a spiritual war that can only be won with spiritual resources, but we've got to know we have these spiritual resources at our disposal, and we've got to use them. God has provided us with everything we need to win the spiritual battles we face, emphasizing that we need to know that, believe it, and act upon it. Sometimes, if you know what to look for, you can "see" something that is invisible; you can see the unseen. It's not a parlor trick, but a valuable spiritual skill. And it's not that difficult if you know what clues to look for. I'd like to show you what those clues are (Koukl, 2017).

Some Christians think of spiritual battle in terms of power encounters with the devil (or demons) where prayer of a certain sort is the principal weapon employed to defeat, or at least to neutralize ("bind"), the powers of darkness. Curiously, Jesus never taught this approach. He never told us to pray to devils (Koukl, 2017). Instead:

Matthew 6:13 - "And lead us not into temptation, but deliver us from the evil one" (**NIV**).

We live in a world made by an invisible Being and this world is thick with invisible things. They are all "around us," in a sense, but not immediately obvious to many since the visible realm is so much more imposing. I am convinced that most Christians do not understand spiritual warfare.

The prophet Elisha's attendant saw something in the visible realm that overwhelmed him, the Syrian army encircling their city with horses and chariots. "Alas, my master!" he said. "What shall we do?"

II Kings 6:15-17 - "When the servant of the man of God got up and went out early the next morning, an army with horses and chariots had surrounded the city. "Oh no, my lord! What shall we do?" the servant asked. "Don't be afraid," the prophet answered. "Those who are with us are more than those who are with them." And Elisha prayed, "Open his eyes, LORD, so that he may see." Then the LORD opened the servant's eyes, and he looked and saw the hills full of horses and chariots of fire all around Elisha" (**NIV**).

Elisha, though, was not shaken. He saw a deeper reality in the unseen realm.

II Kings 6:17 - "And Elisha prayed, and said, LORD, I pray thee, open his eyes, that he may see. And the LORD opened the eyes of the young man; and he saw: and, behold, the mountain was full of horses and chariots of fire round about Elisha" (**KJV**).

Elisha saw something his servant did not see: the enemies of God surrounding the city were themselves surrounded by a massive invisible force arrayed behind the scenes for Elisha's protection.

The prophet is able to see the unseen.

References:

I John 5:19 - "We know that we are of God, and that the whole world lies in the power of the evil one" (**ESV**).

Revelation 12:9 - "And the great dragon was thrown down, the serpent of old who is called the devil and Satan, who deceives the whole world" (**ESV**).

II Corinthians 4:3-4 - "And even if our gospel is veiled, it is veiled to those who are perishing, in whose case the god of this world has blinded the minds of the unbelieving so that they might not see the light of the gospel of the glory of Christ" (**ESV**).

II Timothy 2:24-26 - "The Lord's bondservant must not be quarrelsome, but...patient when wronged, with gentleness correcting those who are in opposition, if perhaps God may grant them repentance leading to the knowledge of the truth, and they may come to their senses and escape from the snare of the devil, having been held captive by him to do his will" (**ESV**).

How do we know that there is a spiritual realm? If we cannot see it, should we believe in it? Many believers and unbelievers today do not want to "deal" with a world we cannot see when the world we do see is hard enough to "deal" with. Before we can discuss the spiritual battle, we have to believe in the spiritual realm. However, if we choose to ignore or not believe in the spiritual realm, we will find ourselves confused, frustrated, and quenching the peace that God has promised to each of us. These verses below describe the spiritual realm and its invisible components?

Nehemiah 9:6 - "And Ezra said: 'Thou art the LORD, thou alone; thou hast made heaven, the heaven of heavens, with all their host, the earth and all that is on it, the seas and all that is in them; and thou preservest all of them; and the host of heaven worships thee'" (**RSV**).

Luke 2:13-15 - "And suddenly there was with the angel a multitude of the heavenly host praising God and saying, 'Glory to God in the highest, and on earth peace among men with whom he is pleased!' When the angels went away from them into heaven, the shepherds said to one another, 'Let us go over to Bethlehem and see this thing that has happened, which the Lord has made known to us'" (**RSV**).

Ephesians 6:12 - "For we are not contending against flesh and blood, but against the principalities, against the powers, against the world rulers of this present darkness, against the spiritual hosts of wickedness in the heavenly places" (**RSV**).

Colossians 1:15-16 - "He is the image of the invisible God, the first-born of all creation; for in him all things were created, in heaven and on earth, visible and invisible, whether thrones or dominions or principalities or authorities, all things were created through him and for him" (**RSV**).

Hebrews 11:3 - "By faith we understand that the world was created by the word of God, so that what is seen was made out of things which do not appear" (**RSV**).

Jesus warned that the devil "is a liar and the father of lies"(**John 8:44, KJV**), employing ruses even Christians are vulnerable to. When we come to Christ, we have a new spirit, true enough, but our minds are still filled with Satan's foolishness, the lies we readily believed that "deceived" and "enslaved" us (**Titus 3:3, KJV**), as we walked "according to the course of this world, according to the prince of the power of the air" (**Ephesians 2:2, KJV**). If you want to see the unseen, look for something spiritually dramatic going on in the visible realm that is so obvious everyone else should see it, but they don't.

For some of us, the hardest battles are fought within ourselves. We can understand the circumstances and situations that the enemy uses to destroy us. We can accept the truth of how the world lures and tempts us. We can understand to some degree that the battle in the spiritual realm is ongoing and real, even though we cannot see it. But, to get a grasp on what is going on within our own hearts and minds can be the hardest, most exhausting, battle of them all.

We suffer in our flesh, whether we feed its desires or deny its pleasures. We are constantly battling between what we want to do versus what we know the Lord wants us to do. "All have sinned and fall short" but the blood of Christ has saved us from destruction. The battle is waged because we are given the power to overcome sin's grasps. There is no battle when there is no opposing side. It takes two to fight. When we are dead in our trespasses, there is no spiritual battle within us because there is no spiritual life. The Spirit of God brings us to life spiritually, yet we live in these bodies of flesh that still have a sinful nature. The battle rages in the lives of believers, but the victory is assured because we are in Christ.

The Bible is also the only book that consistently describes the spirit world without contradictions in a logical, historical manner. It is the one lasting source that has given trustworthy information about the spirit world and has served as a faithful counterweight to the evil spiritual forces. As we mature, we will inevitably notice struggles in our own minds where good and bad thoughts and attitudes battle for dominance to shape behavior. Satan has the power to transmit attitudes and tries to persuade us to do evil.

So, whether we are aware of it or not, a spiritual battle is going on. *a battle for our minds.* The apostle Paul explains how Satan operates by transmitting invisible but powerful negative attitudes:

Ephesians 2:1-3 - "And you he made alive, when you were dead through the trespasses and sins in which you once walked, following the course of this world, following the prince of the power of the air, the spirit that is now at work in the sons of disobedience. Among these we all once lived in the passions of our flesh, following the desires of body and mind, and so we were by nature children of wrath, like the rest of mankind" (**RSV**).

Thankfully, the Bible foretells a future time on earth when Satan will no longer be able to transmit his evil attitudes and the world will finally be at peace:

Revelation 20:2-3 - "And he seized the dragon, that ancient serpent, who is the Devil and Satan, and bound him for a thousand years, and threw him into the pit, and shut it and sealed it over him, that he should deceive the nations no more, till the thousand years were ended. After that he must be loosed for a little while" (**RSV**).

But in the meantime, we must be careful to guard our minds as this unseen spiritual battle rages around us!

We look at our world and rightly wonder, What's going on? We see horrible things happening, suffering and brutality unimaginable to our eyes and senses. We watch terrorist groups rise in the Middle East and Africa, where they brutalize whole populations into fear. They behead and torture captives, showing no shred of decency or humanity. What we are witnessing is pure evil. We are seeing works of *spiritual wickedness* being done *through* men who use religion and politics as coverings for unspeakable acts against their fellow human beings.

The DEVIL is a liar and the father of lies!

CHAPTER 7

WEAPONS OF OUR WARFARE

We're in a battle in this world. We may not see it, we might forget it's there. And the enemy would love nothing more than for us to live unaware, filling our lives with discouragement and defeat, bringing fear and stress, stirring up busyness and strife. If you're a believer living like salt and light in a dark world, you won't go for long without encountering obstacles and attacks that the enemy or evil forces will hurl your direction. But God never leaves us on our own. He equips with all we need to stay aware of Satan's schemes, to live alert in this world, and to stay close to Him

We are told in Scripture, "Is not man forced to labor on earth, And *are not* his days like the days of a hired man" (**Job 7:1, NASB**), a constant battle against the three enemies of our souls: the world, the flesh, and the devil. In our times, especially, the battle is growing in breadth and intensity with each passing day. Spiritual warfare is described in **Second Corinthians** with these words:

II Corinthians 10:3 - "For though we walk in the flesh, we do not war according to the flesh" (**NASB**).

We are "in the flesh" in the sense **verse 3** says that we are human. When it says "we walk in the flesh," it is not talking about sin, but just talking about being human. We can't war, however, "according to the flesh" because our weapons can't be human. It can't be ingenuity or cleverness and it can't be anything contrived by man, no matter our desires.

We have weapons of warfare not of this world

- I have given you authority to trample on snakes and scorpions and to overcome all the power of the enemy; nothing will harm you.

Luke 10:19 - "Behold, I have given you authority to tread on serpents and scorpions, and over all the power of the enemy, and nothing will injure you" (**NASB**).

- Jesus said to him, "Away from me, Satan! For it is written: Worship the Lord your God, and serve him only."

Matthew 4:1-2 - "Then Jesus was led up by the Spirit into the wilderness to be tempted by the devil. And after He had fasted forty days and forty nights, He then became hungry" (**NASB**).

Ephesians 6:10-18 - "Finally, be strong in the Lord and in the strength of his might. Put on the whole armor of God, that you may be able to stand against the schemes of the devil. For we do not wrestle against flesh and blood, but against the rulers, against the authorities, against the cosmic powers over this present darkness, against the spiritual forces of evil in the heavenly places. Therefore take up the whole armor of God, that you may be able to withstand in the evil day, and having done all, to stand firm. Stand therefore, having fastened on the belt of truth, and having put on the breastplate of righteousness, and, as shoes for your feet, having put on the readiness given by the gospel of peace. In all circumstances take up the shield of faith, with which you can extinguish all the flaming darts of the evil one; and take the helmet of salvation, and the sword of the Spirit, which is the word of God, praying at all times in the Spirit, with all prayer and supplication. To that end, keep alert with all perseverance, making supplication for all the saints" (**NASB**).

God is always with us and fights for us:

References

Romans 8:35-39 - "Who shall separate us from the love of Christ? Shall tribulation, or distress, or persecution, or famine, or nakedness, or danger, or sword? As it is written, 'For your sake we are being killed all the day long; we are regarded as sheep to be slaughtered.' No, in all these things we are more than conquerors through him who loved us. For I am sure that neither death, nor life, nor angels nor rulers, nor things present, nor things to come, nor powers, nor height nor depth, nor anything else in all creation, will be able to separate us from the love of God in Christ Jesus our Lord" (**NIV**).

Deuteronomy 31:6 - "Be strong and courageous. Do not fear or be in dread of them, for it is the Lord your God who goes with you. He will not leave you or forsake you" (**NIV**).

Psalm 138:72 - "Though I walk in the midst of trouble, you preserve my life. You stretch out your hand against the anger of my foes; with your right hand, you save me" (**NIV**).

Psalm 37:1-2 - "Do not fret because of those who are evil or be envious of those who do wrong; for like the grass they will soon wither, like green plants they will soon die away" (**NIV**).

Exodus 14:14 - "The Lord will fight for you; you need only to be still" (**NIV**).

Psalm 34:7 - "The angel of the Lord encamps around those who fear him, and he delivers them" (**KJV**).

Isaiah 41:10 - "So do not fear, for I am with you; do not be dismayed, for I am your God. I will strengthen you and help you; I will uphold you with my righteous right hand" (**NIV**).

Isaiah 54:17- "No weapon forged against you will prevail, and you will refute every tongue that accuses you. This is the heritage of the servants of the Lord, and this is their vindication from me, 'declares the Lord" (**NIV**).

Why do we need the armor of God? Satan has always been a formidable enemy. Most often when a Christian refers to his or her "enemies" they are speaking about the sin in their flesh and the temptations and lusts that arise from there. These are enemies because they tempt us to act contrary to the will of God. These can also be spiritual powers such as the spirit of the times which oppose most of mankind, and countless people have succumbed to his attacks and cunning lies. He uses many strategies: from trying to convince us that following our lusts. The desire that we experience that go against God's will. In other words, a desire for anything sinful:

The armor of God, found in **Ephesians 6:10-18**, is made up of the following six items: the belt of truth, the breastplate of righteousness, the shoes of the gospel, the shield of faith, the helmet of salvation and the sword of the spirit. A list and description of the full armor of God can be found below (Smith, 1920).

1. Breastplate of righteousness
2. Shoes of the gospel
3. Shield of faith
4. Helmet of salvation
5. Sword of the spirit
6. Praying
7. How to put on the armor of God

We do not wrestle against flesh and blood

The Bible often illustrates the Christian life as a battle against sin and Satan. We are soldiers of Christ in a spiritual warfare (Smith, 1920).

II Corinthians 10:3-4 - "For though we walk in the flesh, we do not war after the flesh: (For the weapons of our warfare are not carnal, but mighty through God to the pulling down of strong holds)" (**KJV**).

II Timothy 2:3-4 - "Thou therefore endure hardness, as a good soldier of Jesus Christ. No man that warreth entangleth himself with the affairs of this life; that he may please him who hath chosen him to be a soldier" (**KJV**).

Ephesians 6:12 - "As Scripture says, "We do not wrestle against flesh and blood, but against . . . spiritual hosts of wickedness" (**KJV**).

That's why the apostle Paul encourages Christians to "put on the whole armor of God, that you may be able to stand against the wiles of the devil" (**verse 11**). Let's take a look at each piece of this spiritual armor and see how it can enable us to be victorious as soldiers for Christ in our battle against the "spiritual hosts of wickedness."

1. Belt of truth (Ephesians 6:14)

"Stand therefore, having girded your waist with truth," Paul says. Truth is the belt that holds all the other pieces of the armor in place. There are two ways in which truth is a part of the armor of God.

First, it refers to the truths of Scripture as opposed to the lies of Satan. Satan is the father of lies:

John 8:44 - "Ye are of your father the devil, and the lusts of your father ye will do. He was a murderer from the beginning, and abode not in the truth, because there is no truth in him. When he speaketh a lie, he speaketh of his own: for he is a liar, and the father of it" (**KJV**).

John 8:32 - "And ye shall know the truth, and the truth shall make you free" **(KJV)**.

The great truths of the Bible, the love of God, salvation through faith in Jesus Christ, the Second Coming, forgiveness of sin, grace and power to live for Jesus, these truths set us free from Satan's lies.

Satan would have us believe that we are sinful, lost, and without hope. The truth is that God's love and salvation has set us free from sin and death.

The second way that truth serves as a belt, holding together the full armor of God, is our personal commitment to truth. We are to live a life that is upright, transparent, and without deceit. Integrity and honesty are vital to your Christian life. People should know that they can depend on you to be a person of truth and principle.

2.   Breastplate of righteousness (Ephesians 6:14)

The breastplate covers the heart and shields it and the other vital organs. The Bible says, "Keep your heart with all diligence, for out of it spring the issues of life" **(Proverbs 4:23, KJV)**. That is what Christ's righteousness does for you. It protects you against all of Satan's accusations and charges. This righteousness is not made up of the good deeds you do. The Bible is clear that none of us are righteous in ourselves **(Romans 3:10, KJV)**. The breastplate of righteousness is entirely the righteousness of Jesus, which He gives us freely when we accept Him as our Savior:

II Corinthians 5:21 - "For he hath made him to be sin for us, who knew no sin; that we might be made the righteousness of God in him" **(KJV)**.

Ephesians 2:8-9 - "For by grace are ye saved through faith; and that not of yourselves: it is the gift of God: Not of works, lest any man should boast" **(KJV)**.

Philippians 3:9 - "And be found in him, not having mine own righteousness, which is of the law, but that which is through the faith of Christ, the righteousness which is of God by faith:" (**KJV**).

It is Christ's righteousness, not our own righteousness, that covers and protects us.

3.   Shoes of the gospel (Ephesians 6:15)

Soldiers marching into battle must have comfortable shoes. As soldiers of Christ, we must put on "gospel shoes" that will allow us to march wherever our Lord leads. The apostle John says, "He who says he abides in Him [Jesus] ought himself also to walk just as He [Jesus] walked" (**I John 2:6, KJV**). Jesus said, "My sheep hear My voice, . . . and they follow Me" (**John 10:27, KJV**). Satan will try to place obstacles in our path, but in Jesus' strength we can walk forward, following our Lord, obeying Him, and advancing the gospel.

4.   Shield of faith (Ephesians 6:16)

In listing the different pieces of the armor of God, Paul says, "Above all, . . . [take] the shield of faith with which you will be able to quench all the fiery darts of the wicked one" (**Ephesians 6:16, KJV**). When Satan attacks with doubts, the shield of faith turns aside the blow. When temptations come, faith keeps us steadfast in following Jesus. We are able to withstand all the devil's fiery darts, because we know whom we have believed (**II Timothy 3:12, KJV**).

This faith is not something that comes from within us. It is God's gift to us. He gives each of us a measure of faith (**Romans 12:3, KJV**). Then as we walk with Him, that faith grows and develops until it becomes a shield, protecting us and allowing us to live a victorious life in Christ. This was Paul's experience. He said, "I have been crucified with Christ; it is no longer I who live, but Christ lives in me; and the life which I now live in the flesh I live by faith in the Son of God, who loved me and gave Himself for me" (**Galatians 2:20, KJV**). And at the end of that life of faith, he declared, "I have fought the good fight, I have finished the race, I have kept the faith" (**II Timothy 4:7, KJV**). That can be your experience as well, as you use the shield of faith to turn aside everything Satan hurls at you.

5. Helmet of salvation (Ephesians 6:17)

The helmet protects the head, perhaps the most vital part of the body since it is the seat of thought and the mind. When we have a sure knowledge of our salvation, we will not be moved by Satan's deceptions. When we are certain that we are in Christ with our sins forgiven, we will have a peace that nothing can disturb.

Can we be certain of our salvation? Can we be sure? Yes. "If we confess our sins, He is faithful and just to forgive us our sins and to cleanse us from all unrighteousness" (**I John 1:9, KJV**). "God has given us eternal life, and this life is in His Son. He who has the Son has life" (**I John 5:11-12, KJV**).

6. Sword of the spirit (Ephesians 6:17)

The sword of the spirit is the only weapon of offense listed in the armor of God. All the other parts are defensive in nature. God's Word, the Bible, is described as "living and powerful, and sharper than any two-edged sword" (**Hebrews 4:12, KJV**). Jesus used this weapon when Satan tempted Him in the wilderness. To each of Satan's efforts to lead Him into sin, Jesus replied, "It is written. . . ." and proceeded to quote Scripture to destroy Satan's temptations. God's Word is truth (**John 17:17, KJV**). That is why it is so powerful. That is why it is so important that we study the Bible and become familiar with its truths and its power. David wrote, "Your word is a lamp to my feet and a light to my path" (**Psalm 119:105,**

KJV). The sword of God's Word both protects us and destroys our enemy, the devil and his temptations.

7. Prayer (Ephesians 6:18)

Although prayer is not one of the pieces of the whole armor of God, yet Paul closes his list by saying, "Praying always with all prayer and supplication in the Spirit" (**Ephesians 6:18, KJV**). Even when you are clothed with the armor of God, you need to bathe it all in prayer. Prayer brings you into communion and fellowship with God so that His armor can protect you.

How do you put on the whole armor of God?

It isn't as difficult as you might think. All the pieces of the armor are found in a relationship with Jesus. Paul said it like this:

Romans 13:14 - "Put on the Lord Jesus Christ" (**KJV**). When you give yourself to Jesus and "put on" His righteousness, you are clothed in the whole armor of God. Do you sometimes feel weak? Do you find yourself giving in to temptation when you really want to overcome? Are you ever discouraged? We all face these moments. But clothed in the whole armor God, the weakest of His children is more than a match for Satan. With Jesus, clothed in God's invincible armor, you will:

Ephesians 6:10 -11 - "Finally, my brethren, be strong in the Lord, and in the power of his might. Put on the whole armour of God, that ye may be able to stand against the wiles of the devil (**KJV**).

James 1:14 - "But every man is tempted, when he is drawn away of his own lust, and enticed" (**KJV**).

Also called "sin in the flesh." Although the expression "youthful lusts" is often thought of in connection with sinful sexual desires, lusts include anything that go against what is good and right in God's eyes (Smith, 1920).

II Timothy 2:22 - "Flee also youthful lusts: but follow righteousness, faith, charity, peace, with them that call on the Lord out of a pure heart" (**KJV**).

However, he knows what is prophesied about him, that his bitter end is looming.

Revelation 20:10 - "And the devil that deceived them was cast into the lake of fire and brimstone, where the beast and the false prophet are, and shall be tormented day and night for ever and ever" (**KJV**).

If that is, the flesh, the tendency to do evil is in every individual. If you put all these flesh centered, flesh-governed people together in a society, you have what the Bible calls "the world." It is a society governed by the flesh; society, with all the power structures with which we are so familiar with this day, all built upon self-interest. This, any observer of human life can see, pervades the world of our day; self-interest is back of everything.

That is why the revisers have substituted the word "world" here. In a sense, they are right. This is clearly the idea the apostle has in mind. He says, "We are not acting like other people. We do not operate from the same motives; there is something quite different about us. If you try to judge us on the same basis you judge others, you are going to be very far off, you will miss the point entirely. "He is declaring also the fundamental tension in which a Christian lives. He says, "We live in the flesh, in the world of normal society, but we do not fight on those terms. We are not carrying on a worldly war." Perhaps it might be helpful in this connection to review the rendering of certain other versions:

II Corinthians 10:3 - "For though we live in the world, we do not wage war as the world does" (**NIV**).

J. B. Philips puts it this way:

"The truth is that, although of course we lead normal human lives, the battle we are fighting is on the spiritual level" (**Philips**).

The **New English Bible** puts it this way: "Weak men we may be; but it is not as such that we fight our battles" (**NEB**). Perhaps the most helpful is the **Living Letters** translation, which says:

"It is true that I am an ordinary weak human being, but I don't use human plans and methods to win my battles" (**Living Letters**).

It is well expressed in the old hymn:

Where cross the crowded ways of life.
Where sound the cries of race and clan.
Above the noise of selfish strife.
We hear thy voice,
O Son of Man.

We are overcomers in this life because He has overcome. And our lives are hidden in Christ with God. No enemy or obstacle can touch our souls.

We are OVERCOMERS!

CHAPTER 8

THE GOD OF THIS WORLD

The phrase "god of this world" or "god of this age" indicates that Satan is the major influence on the ideals, opinions, goals, hopes and views of the majority of people. His influence also encompasses the world's philosophies, education, and commerce. The thoughts, ideas, speculations and false religions of the world are under his control and have sprung from his lies and deceptions. So, when the Bible says that Satan is the "god of this world," it is not saying that he has ultimate authority. It is conveying the idea that Satan rules over the unbelieving world in a specific way.

In the book of Corinthians:

II Corinthians 4:4 - The unbeliever follows Satan's agenda: "The god of this world has blinded the minds of unbelievers, so that they cannot see the light of the gospel of the glory of Christ" (**NIV**).

Satan's scheme includes promoting false philosophies in the world, philosophies that blind the unbeliever to the truth of the Gospel. Satan's philosophies are the fortresses in which people are imprisoned, and they must be set free by Christ.

Satan and his demons, *the entire spirit world,* in fact, have been a great mystery to this world.

The Apostle Paul revealed the astounding reason why this is the case:

II Corinthians 4:3-4 - "And even if our gospel is veiled, it is veiled to those who are perishing. The god of this age has blinded the minds of unbelievers, so that they cannot see the light of the gospel that displays the glory of Christ, who is the image of God" (**NIV**).

Who is "the god of this world"? Most people would say God, the Creator. But "the god of this world" has *blinded* the minds of people to the gospel of Christ. The god who rules the world is actually Satan the devil.

John 12:31 - "Now is the time for judgment on this world; now the prince of this world will be driven out" (**NIV**).

John 14:30 - "I will not say much more to you, for the prince of this world is coming. He has no hold over me" (**NIV**).

This evil being is called "the prince of this world." We are living in the devil's world!

When Jesus Christ came to Earth, He and Satan engaged in a titanic battle for its future. Had Satan enticed Jesus to sin, He would have failed, and Satan could have ruled the world forever. Christ didn't argue when Satan boasted:

Luke 4:6 - "And he said to him, 'I will give you all their authority and splendor; it has been given to me, and I can give it to anyone I want to'" (**NIV**).

Christ knew that Satan did indeed have charge over the world and its riches.

II Corinthians 4:4 - "The god of this age has blinded the minds of unbelievers, so that they cannot see the light of the gospel that displays the glory of Christ, who is the image of God" (**NIV**).

This passage says the devil blinds people to truth and reality. In fact, he has deceived mankind into believing he doesn't even exist!

Most churchmen today, viewing everything from the perspective of this world today, blindly assume this is God's world. They see certain forces of evil in it, and they feel they must oppose. They see the Christian duty to be that of working to make this a better world. That concept is a wrong viewpoint altogether. This is not a world of God's making. This is Satan's world! Satan is the invisible god of this world. He is the author of its organization, its basic philosophies, its systems of government, business, society, yes, and religions." This is a vitally important truth. Do you recognize the devil's influence in the world over which he is a prince and god today? Or are you one who is blinded to it? The fact that angels and evil spirits are invisible does not negate their existence.

In truth the invisible spirit world is more real than the material and the visible. There is a spirit realm, an invisible dimension of life, that is more real than this physical world we experience with our five senses every day! This spirit realm has more influence on our world, and even in our life, than you realize. In **Ephesians**, Paul told converted Christians:

Ephesians 2:2 - "Wherein in time past ye walked according to the course of this world, according to the prince of the power of the air, the spirit that now worketh in the children of disobedience" (**KJV**).

Believe it or not, Satan works in people, constantly influencing the thoughts and actions of human beings.

Satan moves on the human spirit within people to move them in attitudes of envy, jealousy, resentment, impatience, anger, bitterness and strife. People have no realization of the tremendous power of Satan. The human spirit within each human is automatically tuned to Satan's wavelength. It seems as if Satan has surcharged the air over the entire Earth with his attitude of self-centeredness and vanity. This is an extremely important fact to recognize: Satan broadcasts on our wavelength, and we are automatically tuned in.

How did Satan and the demons come into existence? The biblical revelation on this point is plain, but it must be pieced together from several different passages.

John 1:1-2 - "In the beginning was the Word, and the Word was with God, and the Word was God. The same was in the beginning with God" (**KJV**).

Did God create a devil, and demons? God *did* create angels to help Him create, govern and manage His creation. Angels are ministers, agents and helpers in God's creation. They are servants of God, playing a critical role in fulfilling His eternal purpose. The Bible reveals angelic elders:

Revelation 4:10 - "The four and twenty elders fall down before him that sat on the throne, and worship him that liveth for ever and ever, and cast their crowns before the throne, saying" (**KJV**).

Revelation 19:14 - "And the armies which were in heaven followed him upon white horses, clothed in fine linen, white and clean" (**KJV**).

Psalm 99:1 - "The LORD reigneth; let the people tremble: he sitteth between the cherubims; let the earth be moved" (**KJV**).

The archangel Lucifer was one of just two covering cherubs:

Exodus 25:17-20 - "And thou shalt make a mercy seat of pure gold: two cubits and a half shall be the length thereof, and a cubit and a half the breadth thereof. And thou shalt make two cherubims of gold, of beaten work shalt thou make them, in the two ends of the mercy seat. And make one cherub on the one end, and the other cherub on the other end: even of the mercy seat shall ye make the cherubims on the two ends thereof. And the cherubims shall stretch forth their wings on high, covering the mercy seat with their wings, and their faces shall look one to another; toward the mercy seat shall the faces of the cherubims be" (**KJV**).

In **Ezekiel 28**, God conveys a message to this great angelic being through the Prophet Ezekiel. He refers to Lucifer as "the king of Tyrus."

We know this isn't speaking of a human being: The physical ruler is referred to as "the prince of Tyrus" in **verse 2**; and God describes this "king" in terms that could not possibly apply to a mortal man.

Here is God's message to this spirit being: "Thou sealest up the sum, full of wisdom, and perfect in beauty. Thou hast been in Eden the garden of God; the workmanship of thy tabrets and of thy pipes was prepared in thee in the day that thou wast created. Thou art the anointed cherub that covereth; and I have set thee so: thou wast upon the holy mountain of God; thou hast walked up and down in the midst of the stones of fire" (**verses 12-14**). God created and educated Lucifer for his assignment on Earth's throne, which was placed in the Garden of Eden, before human beings were even created! Lucifer received this special training from the "holy mountain of God," God's throne!

"Thou wast perfect in thy ways from the day that thou wast created," **verse 15** begins. God could not instantaneously create a being of greater talent and beauty than Lucifer. As created, Lucifer was perfect. God did not create the devil! He created a perfect angelic being. But He gave that being free moral agency, the power of choice. The end of **verse 15** reveals what then happened: "till iniquity was found in thee." Lucifer became lawless by sinning against God.

God intended for Lucifer to administer a universe government based on His supreme law of giving, cooperating and serving. But Lucifer thought he could accomplish more by competition, giving rise to sin, violence, destruction, competition, misery and unhappiness. Lucifer became so prideful and arrogant that he attempted to evict God from His throne! In a parallel passage, the Prophet Isaiah revealed the attitude that created the problem: "For thou Lucifer hast said in thine heart, I will ascend into heaven, I will exalt my throne above the stars of God: I will sit also upon the mount of the congregation, in the sides of the north" (**Isaiah 14:13, KJV**)

"When Lucifer allowed thoughts of vanity, jealousy, envy, lust and greed, then resentment and rebellion, to enter and occupy his mind, something happened to his mind!" "His mind became perverted, distorted, twisted! His thinking became warped. God gave him and the angels control over their own minds. They can never straighten them out, never again think rationally, honestly, rightly". Lucifer, the "light bringer", became Satan, the adversary of God and of everything that is good. At that point, God forcefully cast this rebel down (**verses 14-15**):

Ezekiel 28:16 - "By the multitude of thy merchandise they have filled the midst of thee with violence, and thou hast sinned: therefore I will cast thee as profane out of the mountain of God: and I will destroy thee, O covering cherub, from the midst of the stones of fire" (**KJV**).

This catastrophic fall took place probably millions of years before the creation of man.

This great immortal archangel had been placed on Earth to use God's government and laws to prepare to take over the entire universe, but now he and his demons can't roam the heavens at all. In the end time, quite recently, another major spiritual battle took place in which Satan and his demons were again cast down and confined to this Earth. This is described in the important prophetic book of:

Revelation 12:7-9 - "And there was war in heaven: Michael and his angels fought against the dragon; and the dragon fought and his angels, And prevailed not; neither was their place found any more in heaven. And the great dragon was cast out, that old serpent, called the Devil, and Satan, which deceiveth the whole world: he was cast out into the earth, and his angels were cast out with him" (**KJV**).

Here again, this evil spirit being, this "great dragon," is described as he "which deceives the whole world!" What a lightning-bolt statement of his awesome power!

"Therefore rejoice, ye heavens, and ye that dwell in them. Woe to the inhabiters of the earth and of the sea! for the devil is come down unto you, having great wrath, because he knoweth that he hath but a short time" (**verse 12**). Yes, the angels of heaven rejoice over the fact that Satan and his demons are trapped on Earth and can't bother them. But what about us, who inhabit the Earth? To us God says woe! Satan's powerful influence over our world and its affairs has *never* been as strong as it is right now! Demonic activity has never been so intense!

Again, look at the news. Look at our society. Is it possible you are looking at human beings who were created in the image of God, but who are being directly influenced by Satan the devil? Most people do not recognize the influence of evil spirits. That does not change the fact that they are subject to, and continually affected by them. True Christians, however, should not be so ignorant. We must be engaged in daily, regular spiritual *warfare,* resisting these satanic broadcasts.

Ephesians 6:10-12 - "Finally, my brethren, be strong in the Lord, and in the power of his might," the Apostle Paul wrote. "Put on the whole armour of God, that ye may be able to stand against the wiles of the devil. For we wrestle not against flesh and blood, but against principalities, against powers, against the rulers of the darkness of this world, against spiritual wickedness in high places" (**KJV**).

Though Satan and his demons are spiritual and invisible, they routinely seek to aggravate and exploit the human nature, which exists to whatever degree we have come under their sway. Our struggle against these enemies becomes easier with God on our side. Our spiritual lifeline to God is crucial. It is completely *unnatural* for us to think like God. It takes diligent, focused effort to *tune out* of Satan's broadcast and *tune in* to God's wavelength. We must take a stand with God through prayer, Bible study, meditation and fasting (Longman, 2014).

"The awesome human potential, if we care enough about it to *resist* Satan's wiles and evils and discouragements and to persevere in *God's way,* is infinitely superior and higher than Lucifer's, even as created, *before* he turned to rebellion and iniquity!" God protects those whom He will, and empowers His Spirit-begotten people to resist the devil. But what must we do in order to receive this protection and power?

James 4:7-8 - "Submit yourselves therefore to God. Resist the devil, and he will flee from you. Draw nigh to God, and he will draw nigh to you. Cleanse your hands, ye sinners; and purify your hearts, ye double minded" (**KJV**).

What a wonderful promise! What marvelous hope God offers. Understand the reality of the spirit world, utilize your spiritual lifeline, *submit to God,* and fight and conquer Satan!

Ephesians 2:1-3 - "And you hath he quickened, who were dead in trespasses and sins; Wherein in time past ye walked according to the course of this world, according to the prince of the power of the air, the spirit that now worketh in the children of disobedience: Among whom we all had our conversation in times past in the lusts of our flesh, fulfilling the desires of the flesh and of the mind; and were by nature the children of wrath, even as others" (**KJV**).

In our culture, the most commonly accepted form of evidence for proving the existence of something is empirical evidence, which involves using the scientific method of observation and experimentation. Is there empirical evidence for a spiritual realm? It doesn't take much research before one realizes there is "evidence" both for and against the existence of a spiritual realm. It comes down to which studies one wants to believe. The best, and most prevalent, the evidence available proving that there is a spiritual realm is testimonial evidence. We can look at the sheer number of religions around the world and testimonial evidence. Religions around the world and the billions of people who focus their lives on the spiritual realm. Is it likely that so many people would report encounters with the spiritual and it not be real? The best testimonial evidence for a spiritual realm is the Bible itself. Historians, both Christian and non-Christian, agree that the historical authenticity of the Bible is strong. Jesus claimed to be God's Son, the One who came down from heaven. He made this fact quite clear in:

John 8:23 - "And he said unto them, Ye are from beneath; I am from above: ye are of this world; I am not of this world" (**KJV**).

The Bible recounts numerous encounters that people had with the spiritual realm. Jesus cast demons out of people regularly, healed the sick by speaking to them, miraculously fed thousands of people, and spoke with people who should be dead, Moses and Elijah:

Matthew 17:1-3 - "And after six days Jesus taketh Peter, James, and John his brother, and bringeth them up into an high mountain apart, And was transfigured before them: and his face did shine as the sun, and his raiment was white as the light. And, behold, there appeared unto them Moses and Elias talking with him" (**KJV**).

These are all indicators that the spiritual realm is real! We are more than physical entities; we possess a soul/spirit destined for eternity. Even though the spiritual realm is invisible to the physical eye, we are connected to it, and what goes on in the spiritual realm directly affects our physical world. The enemy may be invisible, but he is not fictional. He is very real, and very persistent, waging war against us constantly.

The enemy is invisible, but he is not fictional.

CHAPTER 9

INVISIBLE PLAN

Unseen/Seen

Now the serpent was more crafty than any beast of the field which the Lord God had made. And he said to the woman, "Indeed, has God said, 'You shall not eat from any tree of the garden'?" And the woman said to the serpent, "From the fruit of the trees of the garden we may eat; but from the fruit of the tree which is in the middle of the garden, God has said, 'You shall not eat from it or touch it, lest you die.'" And the serpent said to the woman, "You surely shall not die! For God knows that in the day you eat from it your eyes will be opened, and you will be like God, knowing good and evil."

Genesis 3:1-5 - "Now the serpent was more subtil than any beast of the field which the LORD God had made. And he said unto the woman, Yea, hath God said, Ye shall not eat of every tree of the garden?And the woman said unto the serpent, We may eat of the fruit of the trees of the garden: But of the fruit of the tree which is in the midst of the garden, God hath said, Ye shall not eat of it, neither shall ye touch it, lest ye die. And the serpent said unto the woman, Ye shall not surely die: For God doth know that in the day ye eat thereof, then your eyes shall be opened, and ye shall be as gods, knowing good and evil" (**KJV**).

Man was put in charge of the garden:

Genesis 1:26-31 - "And God said, Let us make man in our image, after our likeness: and let them have dominion over the fish of the sea, and over the fowl of the air, and over the cattle, and over all the earth, and over every creeping thing that creepeth upon the earth. So God created man in his own image, in the image of God created he him; male and female created he them. And God blessed them, and God said unto them, Be fruitful, and multiply, and replenish the earth, and subdue it: and have dominion over the fish of the sea, and over the fowl of the air, and over every living thing that moveth upon the earth. And God said, Behold, I have given you every herb bearing seed, which is upon the face of all the earth, and every tree, in the which is the fruit of a tree yielding seed; to you it shall be for meat. And to every beast of the earth, and to every fowl of the air, and to every thing that creepeth upon the earth, wherein there is life, I have given every green herb for meat: and it was so. And God saw every thing that he had made, and, behold, it was very good. And the evening and the morning were the sixth day" (**KJV**).

So far as we can tell, Satan had no authority, no part in the rule of God over the creation. The chain of command indicated in **chapters 1-3** in **Genesis** is Adam, Eve, and then Satan (as a creature). Satan, in true form, manages to turn this order of authority upside-down. He takes charge, gets to Adam through Eve, and brings about the fall. Satan's arrogance and self-confidence ooze from the verses of our text. The one who wanted to be "like God," and who was cast down because of his pride and ambition:

Isaiah 14:13-14 - "For thou hast said in thine heart, I will ascend into heaven, I will exalt my throne above the stars of God: I will sit also upon the mount of the congregation, in the sides of the north: I will ascend above the heights of the clouds; I will be like the most High" (**KJV**).

Ezekiel 28:2 - "Son of man, say unto the prince of Tyrus, Thus saith the Lord GOD; Because thine heart is lifted up, and thou hast said, I am a God,

I sit in the seat of God, in the midst of the seas; yet thou art a man, and not God, though thou set thine heart as the heart of God:" (**KJV**).

Ezekiel 28:9 - "Wilt thou yet say before him that slayeth thee, I am God? but thou shalt be a man, and no God, in the hand of him that slayeth thee" (**KJV**).

Satan has now convinced Eve that disobedience to God's command will make men "like God".

Genesis 3:5 - "For God doth know that in the day ye eat thereof, then your eyes shall be opened, and ye shall be as gods, knowing good and evil" (**KJV**).

Satan begins with a question, raising doubts about the goodness of God, and ending with a flat denial of God's words which imply that God is a liar. He changes Eve's perspective, so that the God who graciously forbade eating from the forbidden tree is viewed as a God who withholds what is good for man for His own selfish reasons. In the final analysis, Satan seems to achieve a total success by bringing about in men the same rebellion for which he was condemned. Satan approaches Eve as an ally, but in the end he is exposed as her adversary. The fall of man, and its resulting curses, are a direct result of Satan's deception (Deffinbaugh, 2014)

Satan's role in the Book of Job is a kind of microcosm, illustrating the place Satan plays in the overall plan of God. The role Satan plays in Job's life illustrates the role Satan plays in the overall plan of God for creation. Satan is the enemy of God. He is neither humble nor submissive to God. He challenges God, thinking that afflicting Job will result in Job's desertion from the ranks of those who worship God. But God is sovereign in Job's sufferings. Satan can only afflict Job with God's permission and only within the limits God Himself has established.

Job's sufferings, while inflicted by Satan, are ultimately from the hand of God. Job may be asking the wrong questions, but he is asking the right person. After two chapters, Satan passes off the scene. When the story ends, Job's faith has been deepened, and he is worshipping God. Job's final condition is far better than his first. In spite of and because of Satan's opposition, Job has been blessed, and Satan's purpose has been frustrated. In the end, Satan learns nothing and gains nothing. God gained a more intimate relationship with Job, an opportunity to instruct the angels, and an occasion to teach us about Satan, the spiritual war, and the gracious role of suffering in the life of the saint (Deffinbaugh, 2014).

Now there was a day when the sons of God came to present themselves before the Lord, and Satan also came among them. And the Lord said to Satan, "From where do you come?" Then Satan answered the Lord and said, "From roaming about on the earth and walking around on it." And the Lord said to Satan, "Have you considered My servant Job? For there is no one like him on the earth, a blameless and upright man, fearing God and turning away from evil." Then Satan answered the Lord, "Does Job fear God for nothing? Hast Thou not made a hedge about him and his house and all that he has, on every side? Thou hast blessed the work of his hands, and his possessions have increased in the land. But put forth Thy hand, now and touch all that he has; he will surely curse Thee to Thy face." Then the Lord said to Satan, "Behold, all that he has is in your power, only do not put forth your hand on him." So Satan departed from the presence of the Lord:

Job 1:6-12 - "Now there was a day when the sons of God came to present themselves before the LORD, and Satan came also among them. And the LORD said unto Satan, Whence comest thou? Then Satan answered the LORD, and said, From going to and fro in the earth, and from walking up and down in it. And the LORD said unto Satan, Hast thou considered my servant Job, that there is none like him in the earth, a perfect and an upright man, one that feareth God, and escheweth evil? Then Satan answered the LORD, and said, Doth Job fear God for nought? Hast not thou made an hedge about him, and about his house, and about all that he hath on every side? thou hast blessed the work of his hands, and his substance is increased in the land. But put forth thine hand now, and touch all that he hath, and he will curse thee to thy face. And the LORD said unto Satan, Behold, all that he hath is in thy power; only upon himself put not forth thine hand. So Satan went forth from the presence of the LORD" (**KJV**).

Again, there was a day when the sons of God came to present themselves before the Lord, and Satan also came among them to present himself before the Lord. And the Lord said to Satan, "Where have you come from?" Then Satan answered the Lord and said, "From roaming about on the earth, and walking around on it." And the Lord said to Satan, "Have you considered My servant Job? For there is no one like him on the earth, a blameless and upright man fearing God and turning away from evil. And he still holds fast his integrity, although you incited Me against him, to ruin him without cause." And Satan answered the Lord and said, "Skin for skin! Yes, all that a man has he will give for his life. However, put forth Thy hand, now, and touch his bone and his flesh; he will curse Thee to Thy face." So the Lord said to Satan, "Behold, he is in your power, only spare his life."

Job 2:1-6 - "Again there was a day when the sons of God came to present themselves before the LORD, and Satan came also among them to present himself before the LORD. And the LORD said unto Satan, From whence comest thou? And Satan answered the LORD, and said, From going to and fro in the earth, and from walking up and down in it. And the LORD said unto Satan, Hast thou considered my servant Job, that there is none like him in the earth, a perfect and an upright man, one that feareth God, and escheweth evil? and still he holdeth fast his integrity, although thou movedst me against him, to destroy him without cause. And Satan answered the LORD, and said, Skin for skin, yea, all that a man hath will he give for his life. But put forth thine hand now, and touch his bone and his flesh, and he will curse thee to thy face. And the LORD said unto Satan, Behold, he is in thine hand; but save his life" (**KJV**).

These texts contain important truths concerning God, Satan, and man, which we will summarize:

- The Book of Job introduces Satan as an adversary, in the context of suffering, early in the history of mankind.

While Job is not among the very first books of the Bible, many scholars believe Job lived during the patriarchal times, before Moses. While Satan may not be prominent in the Old Testament as a whole, he is clearly introduced early on as God's enemy and man's adversary.

- Satan is counted among the "sons of God" and is thus still included among the angels.
- Satan has freedom to go about the earth and even has access to heaven and the throne of God.
- Satan acknowledges God's authority, but he does not respect it or fully submits to it. Satan knows he cannot afflict Job without God's permission.

Job 1:11 - "But put forth thine hand now, and touch all that he hath, and he will curse thee to thy face" (**KJV**).

Job 2:5 - "But put forth thine hand now, and touch his bone and his flesh, and he will curse thee to thy face" (**KJV**).

- Satan is arrogant toward God. Satan's retort, "Skin for skin," in **verse 4 of chapter 2** may not be fully understood, but the attitude behind it is obvious.

Satan shows no respect for God.

- Satan assumes that men are like him that they strive for success and shun suffering.

Satan's words reveal his belief that men only serve God when it serves their own fleshly interests, and that they will turn from God when suffering comes into their lives. Satan cannot imagine anyone worshipping God for who He is, rather than for what He gives. He thinks men must be bribed to worship and to serve God. His view is: "Take away the success, replace it with suffering, and the saints will turn from God."

- Satan never learns.

Satan is not teachable. Nothing changes his mind. While God acts in a way that could instruct Satan, he neither learns nor changes.

- Unwittingly, Satan serves God's purpose.

Satan's efforts produced the opposite of what he hoped to achieve by inflicting Job with adversity and suffering. While Satan is rebellious toward God and an adversary of Job, the suffering God imposed ultimately resulted in a deepening of Job's faith and brought greater blessings to Job.

Conclusion

As described in the Book of Job, what happened through Satan's opposition to God and Job is exactly what always happens in the plan of God. Satan is allowed to manifest his rebellion and bring about that which he supposes will hinder God's people and His plan. Satan is allowed to do only that which God has planned for His glory and our good. He does nothing apart from divine permission. He does nothing contrary to God's plan. Through Satan's opposition, God's purposes are fulfilled, and

Satan's purposes are frustrated. In spite of his failures, Satan never learns. Instead, he hastens on in his rebellion (Deffinbaugh, 2014)

Unwittingly,

Satan serves God's purpose.

REFERENCES

Bolick, David, *The Unseen World and How It Works*, Activated Magazine, September 2007.

Charisma, Magazine, *Prayers to Win Unseen Battle Raging Against you!*, October 28, 2018.

Deffinbaugh, Bob, *Satan's Part in God's Perfect Plan*, Biblical Studies Foundation, May 17, 2004.

DeJesus, Mark, *Understanding Invisible Things: Heavenly Places*, September 17, 2013.

Eckert, Beth, *Testing Spirits*,WordPress, July 18, 2016.

Got Questions, *What evidence is there of a spiritual realm?*, November 14, 2013.

Howard, Alyssa, *Trust the Unseen: How to Live in Spirit and Truth*. Blog, March 3, 2016.

Jacobs, Cindy, *The Unseen Realm*, Generals International, October 20, 2015.

Kouki, Greg, *The Nature of Spiritual Warfare,* Stand to Reason, July 1, 2017.

Kruse, Dale P., *The Nature of Spiritual Warfare*, December 15, 1999.

Longman, Robert, *Supernatural*, Longman Publishing Group, November 13, 2014.

McMenamin, Cindi, *5 Areas of Your Life Satan Wants to Enter*, Crosswalk, August 9, 2016.

Shirer, Priscilla, *The Truth About Spiritual Warfare and Why It's Important to Pray*, Lifeway, June 2, 2016.

Smith, Johan Oscar, *The whole armor of God, what is it?*, Published in Norwegian by Skjulte Skatt Forlag, May, 1920.

The Holy Bible, *English Standard Version Bible,* (ESV), New York: Oxford University Press, 2009.

The Holy Bible, *King James Version,* (KJV), New York: American Bible Society: 1999.

The Holy Bible, *New American Standard Bible,* (NASB), La Habra, CA: Foundation Publications, for the Lockman Foundation, 1971.

The Holy Bible, *New English Bible, (*NEB), Oxford University Press, 1970.

The Holy Bible, *New International Version,* (NIV), Grand Rapids: Zondervan Publishing House, 1984.

The Holy Bible, *New Living Translation,* (NLT), Tyndale House, Foundation, 2015.

The Holy Bible, *Revised Standard Version Bible,* (RVS), Division of Christian Education of the National Council of the Churches of Christ in the United States of America, 1989.

The Holy Bible, *The New Testament in Modern English,* (Philips), 1958.

Wellman, Jack, *What Are The Gates Of Hell?,* What Christians Want to Know, May 8, 2014.

Wellman, Jacob, *What Does It Mean To Be Seated With Christ in the Heavenly Places?,* November 12, 2014.

Printed in the United States
By Bookmasters